It's Wiggle Time!

by
Marilee Whiting Woodfield

Carson-Dellosa Publishing Company, Inc.
Greensboro, North Carolina

Dedication

To Kira, Tyler, Daniel, and Nathan—
the kids I like to wiggle with the most.

Credits:

Editor: Ashley Futrell
Layout Design: Mark Conrad
Inside Illustrations: Janet Armbrust
Cover Design: Peggy Jackson
Cover Illustration: Dan Sharp

ISBN 1-59441-041-0

Table of Contents

Introduction 4

Incorporating Music into Movement Activities 5-6

Make Your Own Music 7-9

Any Time Is Wiggle Time 10

All About Me 11-12

Alphabet 13-14

Balloons 15-16

Balls 17-18

Body Parts 19-23

Bugs and Other Crawling Things 24-26

Colors 27-28

Community Helpers 29-30

Emotions 31

Food 32-33

Friends 34-35

Holidays 36-40

Numbers 41-42

On the Farm 43-45

Opposites 46-47

Seasons 48-58

Shapes 59-61

Space 62-64

Sports 65-66

Transportation 67-69

Weather 70-73

Zoo Animals 74-79

Music Selection Collection 80

Introduction

Anyone who has worked with young children can attest to their boundless energy. The challenge for teachers and caregivers is to channel that energy appropriately.

It's Wiggle Time! is a compilation of theme-based activities to help you incorporate movement and music into the curriculum. Music and movement activities are not only useful for getting the wiggles out, they also help children master gross motor skills and coordination while relieving stress and tension. Additionally, skills such as self-expression, sequencing, auditory discrimination, balance, and many others are built right into these activities. So, learning is an intrinsic part of the fun and becomes a great motivator, not only for the current activity, but for future movement and fitness learning, as well!

The first section of *It's Wiggle Time!* is a compilation of ideas to help you incorporate music into the movement curriculum. It gives you encouragement and confidence in using music in the classroom and includes suggestions for enhancing the movement experience with music.

It's Wiggle Time! also includes a short section of quick wiggling and transition ideas to move from one activity to the next, or for fill-in activities when a little extra wiggle time is needed.

The majority of *It's Wiggle Time!* is a collection of activities to help you use movement with the most popular classroom themes. With a little creativity, these activities can be manipulated to fit any theme you explore.

Remember, imagination is the limit. Movement is beneficial in so many ways. Enjoy the uninhibited movement of the children around you—they just might teach you a thing or two!

Almost all of the activities in *It's Wiggle Time!* are cooperative. The reward of movement is in participating—not in finishing first. Wherever possible, work in teams and race against the clock or past performances instead of each other. Give praise for effort. Feeling good and trying hard are their own rewards in wiggling activities.

Regardless of how you incorporate movement and music into lessons, you will find your time spent in a worthwhile manner because wiggling is an important part of every child's day. Developing a love of movement creates happy and confident children. A love of movement brings a lifetime of benefits. Health and fitness, self-esteem, and confidence are just the beginning. Stretch, warm-up—now, let's get wiggling!

Incorporating Music into Movement Activities

Our bodies are tuned to music; it is all around us every day. Some of it is rhythmic (like a washing machine), melodic (like a doorbell), or even chaotic (like rush hour traffic). Music elicits thoughts and feelings, and these can often be translated into movement.

Have you ever noticed that most people become relaxed and even a little bit sleepy during a lullaby or a little rowdy when they hear hard rock music? You can influence students' moods and the classroom tempo with music. Play music often in the classroom; use it to excite, enthuse, calm, and relax students.

The quickest, cheapest, and easiest way to incorporate music in the classroom is to sing! So, you're not an opera star? Children don't care. Simple and repetitive words to familiar tunes will result in a quicker response than complex scores and poetic verse. For example, to the tune of "Here We Go Looby Loo," repeatedly sing, "Children pick up your toys." Not only will the class start picking up toys, they will also begin singing with you!

Pitch, Timbre, Tempo, and Volume

To add some variety when you sing, change the pitch, timbre, tempo, and volume to hold the class's attention. *Pitch* refers to how high or how low you sing. *Timbre* is the identifying "voice" you use. (This is what makes a duck sound like a duck and a clarinet sound like a clarinet.) *Tempo* is how fast or how slow the music is. And *volume*, of course, determines how loud or how soft you sing. You can use any combination of these or focus on just one area to add interest to a song.

Chant

Chanting is another musical alternative. Rather than using a singing voice, chant or say a word instead (color words, for instance). Repeat it over and over again. Now, divide the group into two teams. Tell team one to continue to chant the first word and have the second team chant a second word. Add a rhythm instrument to the beat of the chant. Explain to students that they are chanting in a round!

Listen and Move

Gather three or four selections of music, each with a different tempo. Have children lie on the floor and listen while you play each selection. Ask if the music reminds them of something else. Perhaps it makes them think of birds flying or elephants stomping. Now, have them stand up while you replay the music. Encourage them to move in a way that matches the music. They should feel inspired to move quickly whenever the tempo is rapid and slowly and methodically whenever the tempo drags.

Variation: Obtain a keyboard and have children dance and move to the many varied tones, timbres, and rhythms that can be created.

Selection Collection.

Build a music library with various selections so that you have lots of choices during movement activities. Be sure to include current popular performers, "oldies," and classical selections, as well as selections that are both globally and culturally diverse. Play music from each genre and have children vote for their favorites and least favorites. Use the music library in the many movement experiences you have each day. See page 80 for a list of selections to get your collection started.

Listening for Music.

Hang a sheet or place a large obstacle between yourself and the class so that they can hear you but cannot see you. Tell them that you will be making music with ordinary things, and you want them to guess what you are using.

Suggestions: Crumple paper, pour water into a tin pie pan, tap with a pencil, etc.

Echo.

Have children lie on their backs so that they can hear you but cannot see you. Use your voice to create a unique sound. For example, sing each child's name in an operatic style or cluck her name like a chicken. Now, have children try to echo your voice. Continue calling and echoing, and invite children to take turns creating their own echoes.

Music and Art.

Inspire students to create works of art using a variety of music and mixed media. Tell them that they can use their whole arms to paint or use crayons or chalk to color with their toes. They can draw small and tight and then make big swooshes as though they are conducting the music. Suggest making dots of paint for staccato notes and long lines for long, drawn-out music. A student could even color on a very small piece of paper with a sharpened crayon or paint large swooshes with a big paintbrush on a mural. After students complete the work, have them step back to see if they recognize the songs from their paintings. Note the music, display the work, and start your own musical classroom museum of art!

Make Your Own Music

Caution: Some small objects may present choking hazards and are not appropriate for children under age three.

Musical Instruments . . . .

If you do not already have a classroom set, you can make your own instruments with simple materials and recycled objects.

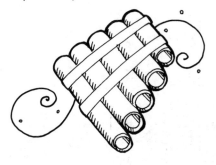

Panpipes: Gather several straws or plastic aquarium tubing (found at pet shops or home improvement stores in the plumbing section). Cut five pieces—6" (15 cm), 5½" (14 cm), 5" (13 cm), 4½" (11½ cm), and 4" (10 cm) long, respectively. Lay them on the table so that the bottoms of the straws are lined up in a straight row. Tape across the straws along the bottom and then again near the top of the shortest straw. To play, a student should hold the panpipes so that the straight edge is against his lips and hum across the straws.

Tambourines: Place two heavy-duty paper or foam plates together with the rims touching each other. Punch 6–10 holes around the outside edges of the plates. If desired, put some gravel, rice, or dried beans between the plates. Glue them together along the edges. Thread a jingle bell onto a short piece of chenille craft stick and pass it through one set of holes on the plates. Twist the chenille craft stick to hold it in place. Repeat for the other holes. To play, a student should shake the tambourine in the air or pat it against a hip.

Maracas: Any empty containers (yogurt container, plastic soda bottle, tin can, etc.) can be used for maracas. Place a small handful of gravel, rice, or dried beans in the container. Seal the top closed with tape. To play, shake or rock the maraca back and forth. Experiment with different containers or contents to make various different maraca sounds.

Horns: Gather a 1' piece (30½ cm) of ½" (1½ cm) plastic aquarium tubing. Slip the end of the tube over the end of a funnel and secure with a piece of electrical or duct tape. Make several horns using various funnel sizes. To play, a student should press lips together and blow hard through the tube or hum into it.

Sand Blocks: Obtain at least two small wooden blocks, each approximately 2" x 3" (5 cm x 7½ cm). Glue or tape sandpaper to the blocks, completely covering one side of each block. To play, a student should rub the sandpaper sides of the blocks together.

Sticks: Use chopsticks, twigs, or unsharpened pencils for rhythm sticks. To play, a student should tap the sticks together or tap them on various objects (floor, chair, wooden block, etc.).

Dryer Hose: Cut several pieces of plastic dryer hose in 6" (15 cm) increments, ranging from 2' (61 cm) to 5' or 6' (1½ m or 2 m). Cover the ends of the hoses with tape to protect fingers from jagged edges. To play, a student should bang the hose on the ground while moving it like an undulating snake.

Banjos: Create a banjo using rubber bands, a cardboard tube, and a tissue box. Make a hole in one end of the tissue box and insert a cardboard tube. Secure with glue or tape. Remove the plastic barrier that covers the hole in the box. Slide three or four different-sized rubber bands over the hole. To play, a student should pluck or strum the rubber bands.

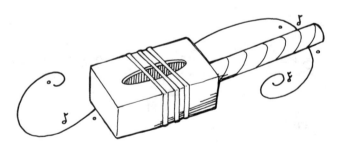

‹∧∧›

Bands . . . .

Now that you have several different instruments, you can start a classroom band! Have students take turns so that each child has the chance to play every instrument while marching around the room or the school. Vary the tempo and the rhythm while marching. Give everyone the opportunity to be the drum major (the one who leads the band). When they get the hang of it, you can start a classroom band with all kinds of things.

Kitchen Band: When you start exploring, you will find lots of ways for students to make music using kitchen items. Here are some instructions to get them started. Have students:

* drum on pots and pans with various utensils, such as gravy stirrers, wire whisks, rubber spatulas, or wooden spoons.
* tap different utensils together (wooden spoons, several teaspoons stacked on top of each other, etc.).
* stroke a wire cooling rack with a fork or wire whisk.
* shake a bowl filled with dried beans or rice.
* tap two cups together or tap the cups on the ground.
* clang two pot lids together like cymbals or tap a lid on a pot.
* hold the ring that connects measuring spoons or cups together, and jingle the spoons or cups.
* scrape the inside of a metal bowl with a wire whisk.

Recycling Band: Have everyone bring in some clean, recyclable items and use them to create a band. Students can:

* crumple newspaper or copy paper by holding on to each side and compressing and expanding the paper to the beat.
* play the soda cans. First, tie a bunch of tin cans together with a string. Have a student hold the string while jangling and clanging the cans together.
* blow across the mouth of an empty water bottle. Or, you can fill bottles with different amounts of water to create different tones when the instruments are played.
* tap empty boxes together like cymbals.

Body Band: Bodies can make music, too. Have students:

* stomp their feet.
* clap their hands.
* pat their bellies.
* make rhythmic noises with their mouths.
* snap their fingers.
* cup their hands and squeeze them together to expel air quickly.

‹∧∧›

 CD-104041 *It's Wiggle Time!*

Any Time Is Wiggle Time

It is not often that you can get through an entire circle time without needing to pause to get the wiggles out. Occasionally, you may have to wait for another class to vacate the room you are using next, or you may have a few minutes to fill before moving to the next activity. All of these times, and probably many more, are great times for transition ideas and wiggle time activities to keep children from becoming too restless and distracted. *Transitioning* is a fancy word for getting from one place to another (or from one activity to another) without losing anyone. As any teacher knows, these times can be especially challenging. When you find something that works and use it consistently, it will often take little more than a simple verbal cue for children to know exactly what you want them to do. For example, when you use the same song every day to signal time to clean up, children will automatically know what you want them to do when they hear the first notes of the song.

Little Hands

The toughest aspect of transitioning is getting children's attention. After you get their attention, finding something to do with their hands is key to keeping them focused. Try various activities and positions to keep those busy little hands happily engaged. Favorite finger plays, using imaginary glue to attach hands to heads (or somewhere else), clapping, swimming, etc., are all great ways to redirect children and their attention.

Walk This Way

When walking as a group, try working together to get from one place to the other.
- ❀ Instruct students to hold hands and make a long, hissing snake.
- ❀ Have them pretend to be a train of elephants. Tell each child to grab the tail (hand) of the elephant in front of her with her trunk (hand). Let students swing tails and trunks back and forth as they roam.
- ❀ Make a movement (such as raising your hand) and have them mimic it in rounds like doing the wave.
- ❀ Show students how to stand close together, pump their arms, and make chugging noises as they "Choo-choo!" to the next room.

Wiggle Ideas

Use these fun wiggle activities to get the wiggles out and bring everyone back into focus.
- ❀ **Wiggle Stretch:** Choose a body part. Have students wiggle them ferociously, stretch them as far as possible, then bring them back in close.
- ❀ **Jackhammer:** Let students jump up and down quickly as though working a jackhammer on the pavement. At your signal, work should stop. At the next signal, begin working again.
- ❀ **Creepy-Crawly:** Instruct students to move their fingers like caterpillars. Have them slowly climb from their toes all the way to their heads and back down to their toes again.
- ❀ **Piano Man:** Let students sing a favorite song while playing air piano (guitar, drum, etc.) to the music. Be sure to tell them to end the impromptu performance with big bows.

All About Me

My Name Is

Using the tune of the old alphabet chant, "My name is Annie, and my boyfriend's name is Albert. We come from Alabama, and we sell apples," help each child create a personalized chant using her name, a friend's name, a favorite activity, and her favorite color.

> ***Sample:***
> My name is: Sierra
> My friend's name is: Dawn
> I like to: play baseball
> My favorite color is: green

Have the chosen student bounce a ball on each beat of the chant. (See if she can bounce it under her legs, too.) The chant would now go: "My name is Sierra, and my friend's name is Dawn. I like to play baseball, and my favorite color is green." Have all of the children repeat the chant together and continue until everyone has had a turn to be highlighted. For an easier activity, let students pass balls between partners to the beat of the chant. Or, simply let them clap to the beat.

Roll the Ball

Have students sit in a circle with their legs spread apart so that each child's feet are touching the feet of the children sitting on either side of him. Give a ball to one child to hold between his legs. Instruct him to roll the ball to someone who has brown hair, an orange shirt, braids, a hat, or some other distinguishing characteristic. Continue rolling and passing the ball until everyone has had a turn.

Variation: Have children sit in the circle as above, only this time, have them pay compliments to the recipients as they roll the ball. Encourage them to be as specific as possible. For instance, the first child might roll the ball across the room to Jennifer and say, "I like Jennifer because she always shares with me." Encourage Jennifer to acknowledge the compliment by saying, "Thank you." Jennifer then, in turn, compliments and rolls the ball to another child until everyone has been included.

Look What I Can Do!

Write each child's name on a word strip or index card. Have students sit or stand in a circle so that everyone can see each other. Draw a name from the stack to select a leader. Have her say, "Look what I can do!" and then perform some action, such as jumping jacks, a somersault, standing on tiptoes, etc. Have everyone else in the class repeat the action and have the leader draw another name. Continue until everyone has had the opportunity to participate.

Variation: Play "Look What I Can Do!," only this time add on and repeat each child's activity in succession. For example, if John does a somersault, and then Joseph does a twirl, the class would twirl, then somersault. If Susanna jumps as high as she can, the class would jump, twirl, and then somersault. Continue adding an action as you go around the circle until everyone has had a chance to participate.

Spotlight Dance

Write each child's name on a word strip or index card. Turn off the lights and play a favorite selection of music. Encourage all of the children to dance or move to the music in any way they want. Select a name from the stack. Illuminate the card with a flashlight so that all of the children can see it. Have the child come to the front of the room while you hold the flashlight over his head to spotlight him while he dances. While you spotlight him, announce his name and any other unique characteristics that you know about him. For instance, while spotlighting Chad say, "This is our friend Chad. He likes to color, read books, and run on the playground. He has brown hair and is wearing a striped shirt." Have all of the children applaud Chad and continue dancing while you choose another child to spotlight. If desired, have children stop dancing and mimic the selected child's dance moves. Continue until everyone has been spotlighted.

Extension: Let children take turns holding the flashlight to highlight the different dancers in the classroom. Be sure to warn them to avoid shining the light directly into anyone's eyes.

Mirror Me

Obtain three full-length mirrors so that children can see themselves move from more than one angle at a time. If obtaining three mirrors is not possible, one will be sufficient. Set up the mirrors like a dressing room with one mirror flat against the wall and the other two angled out to the sides. You can create hinges between the mirrors with duct tape. Secure the center mirror to a wall or a piece of sturdy classroom furniture.

Have each child spend a few minutes in front of the mirrors exploring their faces and bodies and how they look when they move. Encourage children to move slowly and choose a full range of poses. Have them make faces and glance at their reflections from the side.

Plain Old Me! (finger play)

Sing or chant "Plain Old Me!" as you perform the finger play with students.

Plain Old Me!

I have 10 fingers.	*(wiggle fingers)*
I have 10 toes.	*(wiggle toes)*
I have two hands, and two ears, and a nose.	*(shake hands, touch ears, and point to nose)*
I have some hair,	*(place hands on head)*
And a face you see,	*(open hands on the sides of cheeks around face)*
But the best thing I have . . .	
Is plain old me!	*(point to chest)*

CD-104041 *It's Wiggle Time!*

Alphabet

Alphabet Hop

Create alphabet cards by writing or printing large alphabet letters, each on a separate sheet of paper or card stock. You may want to laminate these pages for durability.

Tape the alphabet letters to the floor in a large circle. Have children stand on the letters around the circle. Play some lively music and have them jump from letter to letter. When the music stops, have each child land and stay on a letter. Select one child and have her identify the letter, its sound, or something that begins with that letter. Continue hopping and recognizing until each child has had a turn.

Variation: Make a second set of identical letters and attach them to a wall or bulletin board. When the music stops, select a child and have him pick up the letter he is standing on. Instruct him to tape his letter over the matching letter on the wall. After taking his turn, he should return to the circle. Continue playing until all of the letters have been matched and everyone has had a turn.

Singing Letters

Make a poster of the alphabet letters in large script so that children can easily see it. Sing the alphabet song as you point to each letter.

Repeat the song using various tempos or voices. For instance, students might whisper, yell like baseball umpires, sing really fast, act very sleepy, etc. To really wake them up, try singing the song backward!

When the song is mastered, cut squares of construction paper big enough to cover one letter at a time on the poster. Cover four or five letters and sing the alphabet song again, this time inserting a word or sound (clap, "Yee-haw!," sniff, etc.) in place of the hidden letters.

Alphabet Dash

Write each letter of the alphabet on an index card or sturdy piece of card stock. Spread the cards faceup around a large play area. Select one child to go first. At your signal, she should dash off to find the letter that you specify. For added fun, instruct students to bring the letter cards to you in funny ways (walking like a gorilla, hopping like a bunny, etc.). Continue dashing, finding, and returning until all of the students have had a chance to play.

Extension: Add two or three more cards for often used letters (R, S, T, vowels, etc.) Select several students and give them each a letter assignment from a word. For example, send three children to find the letters in the word *pig*. When children dash back with the letters, demonstrate how the letters make a word. Sound out each letter and read the completed word together. Repeat with other simple words, such as *car*, *dog*, *cat*, etc.

Extension: For a real challenge, have fun with some "big words." Select eight students to find the letters in the word *flamingo*. When students have the letters, tell them to stand in order, holding up the cards. First, help students try to sound out the big word. Then, describe the definition without saying the word. If they still need help guessing the word, show them a picture of the item. Finally, act out the "big word" together. Some other funny words to try are *ostrich, umbrella, poodle, banana*, etc.

Body Letters

Have children attempt to make all of the letters of the alphabet by bending, twisting, and moving their bodies. For example, if they raise their hands over their heads and spread out their arms, they can make the letter T.

Next, have children work in teams to build the letters. For example, to make the letter A, have two children lie on the floor at an angle with their heads together. Let a third child lie across the middle of the other two to make the cross bar. Encourage students to try to make both uppercase and lowercase body letters.

Alphabet Maze

Make a maze of letters for children to step from one letter to the next in alphabetical order. Using the alphabet cards you created for the "Alphabet Hop" activity (page 13), tape the letters on the ground in a pattern similar to the one shown below. Starting on the letter A, have children move through the maze, stepping on the letters in order until they come to the letter Z. For an added challenge, have students balance on one foot on each letter, hop like a frog from letter to letter, or start with the letter Z and go backward through the alphabet until they reach the letter A.

Extension: Ask students to say a word or make a sound that starts with each letter before they move on to the next letter.

Extension: To make the maze more complicated, add extra spaces with random letters, numbers, or instructions, such as "Wrong Way," "Go Back," or "Try Again."

Balloons

Warning: Before completing any balloon activity, ask parents about possible latex allergies. Also, remember that uninflated or popped balloons may present a choking hazard.

Balloon Bop

Provide each child with an inflated balloon. You may want to write each child's name on her balloon with a permanent marker to avoid confusion. Play a favorite music selection and have children grab the ends of their balloons. Allow students to bop balloons in the air in various ways to the beat of the music. Let students bop them high, low, with friends, on the head, against the feet, with other body parts, back and forth between the hands, fast, slow, etc. Have children take turns leading the rest of the class in bopping form.

Extension: Suspend a piece of string across the room by tying or taping it between two chairs. Let students use tennis rackets (see activity on page 65) to bop balloons back and forth over the "net." See who can keep her balloon suspended in the air the longest.

Balloon Relay

Divide the group into small teams of four or five children. Give each team an inflated balloon. Mark a starting line with chalk or tape. Place a second line about 20' (6 m) away. Divide each team so that there are team members standing behind both lines. At your signal, have the first person on each team place the balloon between his knees and waddle to the other line to hand it off to a waiting team member. If the balloon is dropped, the player must stop and reposition it before moving forward. Play continues until all teams have completed the relay.

Extension: Do the relay again, this time using different body parts and skills for carrying the balloons. For instance, let students place balloons between the ankles and move by jumping forward, or have two team members work together to keep a balloon between their shoulders. You can also have two children link arms and place a balloon between their backs as one child walks forward and the other walks backward.

Variation: Fill the balloons with water for some outdoor relay fun on field day.

Secret Messages

On several small slips of paper (at least one per child), write simple activities, such as "Jump up and down 10 times," "Spin in a circle 5 times," "Do 12 jumping jacks," etc. Fold the slips and put them inside uninflated balloons. Blow up the balloons and tie knots in them. Be careful not to inhale the slips of paper.

Place all of the balloons in a large garbage bag or other container. Ask children to take turns selecting balloons. One at a time, have them pop their balloons (by sitting or stomping on them) and then lead the class in performing the secret message activities inside. Make sure that everyone helps to pick up all of the broken balloon pieces when you finish.

ΛΛΛΛΛΛΛΛΛΛΛΛΛΛΛΛΛΛΛΛΛΛΛΛΛΛΛΛΛΛΛΛΛΛΛΛΛΛΛΛΛΛΛΛ

Balloon Boxing.

This is a great activity for relieving frustration. Obtain one helium-filled balloon for each child. Securely tape the balloon strings to the floor or the edges of tabletops. Make sure there is plenty of space between students. Play some upbeat boxing music, such as "Eye of the Tiger" by Survivor (*Survivor: Greatest Hits*, Scotti Bros., 1993), and let students begin punching away. Show children how to shuffle back and forth between punches like a boxer. Let students try punching to the beat or using a pattern (left, right, right, left, right, right, etc.).

Group Balloon.

Have students sit in a circle as you blow up a balloon and tie a knot in it. Have one child describe what happens to the balloon as you fill it with air. (The balloon stretches and expands.) Now, take a sharp object and pop the balloon. Have children describe what happens. (Broken pieces fly everywhere; it makes a loud noise; etc.) Blow up a second balloon, this time pinching the neck closed without tying it. Have another child describe what happens when you blow up the second balloon. Now, release it and have another child explain what happens. (The air leaks out, and the balloon flies around unpredictably while making a funny noise.)

Tell the class that they are going to be a "group balloon" today. Have them stand in a circle and join hands. Next, have children crowd close together while continuing to hold hands. Explain that they are now just like an uninflated balloon. Encourage everyone to blow hard to increase the size of the balloon. Have students continue blowing and taking small steps backward until the group balloon is completely inflated and their arms are stretched as far apart as possible. Pretend to tie a knot in the end of the balloon. Now, pretend to pop the balloon with a big pin and have children drop hands, jump in the air, and fall quickly to the ground. Repeat several times allowing different children to pretend to pop the group balloon.

Begin the balloon experience again, with students blowing and expanding the circle. This time, pretend to pinch the neck of the balloon with your fingers instead of tying a knot. Have children watch your fingers closely. When you open them, the air will begin rushing out of the group balloon, and the group will "fly" in all sorts of random directions. Repeat to allow different children to pinch and release the balloon. Be sure that there is plenty of open space for all of the members of the group balloon to safely fly around the play area.

Crazy Balloons.

What happens when you put a small rubber ball inside a balloon? Slip a ball into an uninflated balloon. Blow up the balloon and tie it securely. Have the class stand in a circle. Toss the balloon to a student. Have students pass it around. Next, try "bouncing" the balloon from student to student. Have children describe (and even mimic) the balloon's crazy movements.

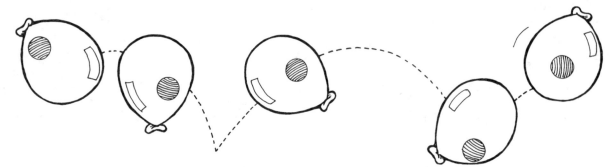

ΛΛΛΛΛΛΛΛΛΛΛΛΛΛΛΛΛΛΛΛΛΛΛΛΛΛΛΛΛΛΛΛΛΛΛΛΛΛΛΛΛΛΛΛ

Balls

Body Bounce

How many ways can students dribble or bounce balls? Probably a lot more ways than they ever thought! Depending on children's developmental levels, you may want to use beach balls or soft foam balls for this activity. Begin by telling students to bounce the balls and catch them between beats. Now, have them bounce the balls to the beat while singing "The Bouncing Song" to the tune of "Row, Row, Row Your Boat."

The Bouncing Song
Bounce, bounce, bounce the ball.
Bouncing's so much fun!
Bouncing, bouncing, bouncing, bouncing,
5–4–3–2–1!

When they get the hang of it, challenge them to try to bounce the balls with their:
- ❀ elbows.
- ❀ foreheads.
- ❀ knees.
- ❀ fingertips.
- ❀ feet while sitting on the floor.
- ❀ feet while standing.

Explore other ways to bounce the balls while singing "The Bouncing Song."

Variation: Instead of dribbling with different body parts, let students bounce beach balls or soft foam balls off different body parts. Have children stand a few feet away from you. Call out a child's name and a body part. Have the child move in front of the class and try to bounce a ball off the named body part.

Bounce by Bounce

Everyone will need a rubber playground ball for this activity. Depending on the developmental levels of the class, you may want to use beach balls or lightweight bouncing balls for this activity. If there are not enough balls for each child to have her own, adapt the activity to work in pairs. Instruct children that they should mimic your bounces as closely as possible. (This also means *not* bouncing when you are *not* bouncing.) Warm up by bouncing the ball to a steady beat. Encourage students to try to mimic you during the warm-up activity. Now, bounce a little faster, and faster still. Then, slow it down and stop. Now that everyone is warmed up, tell children to watch and listen.

Bounce your ball once and then catch it. Have the children mimic your bounce. Next, let your ball bounce twice before catching it. Again, have children mirror your activity. Now, throw your ball into the air and catch it without letting it hit the ground. Have children try. Continue patterns of bouncing and catching. Divide the group into smaller teams and have them take turns leading each other in the bouncing activity.

ᐱᐱᐱᐱᐱᐱᐱᐱᐱᐱᐱᐱᐱᐱᐱᐱᐱᐱᐱᐱᐱᐱᐱᐱᐱᐱᐱᐱᐱᐱᐱᐱᐱᐱᐱᐱ

Ball Obstacle Course . . . .

Set up a fun obstacle course utilizing many ball skills. Some suggested obstacles and skills tests might include:

* balancing balls on backs while crawling a short distance.
* passing balls through a hoop.
* bouncing balls over a barrier, such as a sawhorse or chair.
* rolling balls to knock over a stack of cans.

Time students as they go through the course. Have each child try to beat his time on his second attempt.

Quick and Easy Activities . . . .

Try these exciting activities for quick transitions, fun, and relaxation.

* Practice balance and stretching. Using a large workout ball, have children take turns lying across the ball on their backs or stomachs. You and an adult volunteer should help each child balance as you rock the ball back and forth.
* Roll a ball to a child to have him transition into another activity or to signify that it is his turn to answer a question or share a thought.
* Obtain several large playground balls with handles. Let students have a bouncing race.
* Set up a course of several hoops and baskets of various sizes. See how quickly students can score by tossing a ball through each hoop and into each basket.
* Let students practice throwing or kicking balls using nondominant hands or feet.
* Have students experiment with a variety of balls of different sizes, weights, materials, bouncing capabilities, etc. Ask, "Which ones bounce the best? Which ones are best for kicking? Which ones are easiest to throw? Do bigger balls roll faster than smaller balls? Which balls bounce the highest?" Some suggested balls to use are soft foam balls, small rubber balls, table tennis balls, soccer balls, basketballs, baseballs, tennis balls, footballs, hollow plastic balls with holes in them, playground balls, beach balls, etc.

ᐱᐱᐱᐱᐱᐱᐱᐱᐱᐱᐱᐱᐱᐱᐱᐱᐱᐱᐱᐱᐱᐱᐱᐱᐱᐱᐱᐱᐱᐱᐱᐱᐱᐱᐱᐱ

Body Parts

This Is My . . . .

Have children sit in a circle with you so that everyone can see each other. Tell children that you will begin by pointing to and naming different body parts. If you correctly identify a body part, children should clap and stand up in agreement. If you incorrectly identify a body part, children should sit, fold their arms across their chests, and shake their heads in disagreement.

For example, point to your nose and say, "This is my nose." Children should stand up and clap in agreement. Have all of the children point to their noses and say, "This is my nose." Next, point to your ear and say, "This is my knee." Recognizing that this statement is incorrect, children should sit, fold their arms, and shake their heads in disagreement.

Have one child help you point to the correct body part.
Have all of the children point to their knees and say, "This is my knee."
If you wish, choose students to take turns leading the class in this activity.

All of My Body Parts Together Make Me! . . . .

Instruct children to wiggle or point to each body part as they sing or chant the following rhyme.

All of My Body Parts Together Make Me!
These are my fingers,
These are my toes.
This is my hair,
And this is my nose.
These are my shoulders,
And this is my knee.
All of my body parts
Together make me!

These are my hands,
And these are my hips.
This is my back,
And these are my lips.
This is my leg,
And my eyes help me see.
All of my body parts
Together make me!

ΛΛΛΛΛΛΛΛΛΛΛΛΛΛΛΛΛΛΛΛΛΛΛΛΛΛΛΛΛΛΛΛΛΛΛΛΛΛΛΛΛΛΛΛΛΛΛΛΛΛ

Body Glue

Make copies of the Body Parts Cards (pages 22–23). Color, cut out, and laminate the cards as desired.

Place all of the Body Parts Cards in a hat or box and mix them. You may want to remove cards for body parts that are above the shoulders. Draw two cards from the hat. Tell children that today you have special body glue. Whichever body parts you draw from the hat will be "glued" together. Each time a new set of body parts is drawn from the hat, the glue can be separated to create a new bond. For example, if the knee and elbow cards are drawn, children must glue their elbows to their knees and stay that way until you tell them to break the bond and get ready for the next set of cards.

Extension: Have children work together as partners. This time, the bond of glue cannot be broken. Draw two cards from the hat—for example, the hand and the foot. One partner glues his hand to the other partner's foot. Draw two more cards—the elbow and the head this time, for example. Again, one partner glues his elbow to the other's head, being careful not to break the existing bond between the hand and the foot. Continue playing until all of the children are completely glued together.

Variation: For a challenge, specify right or left for paired body parts, such as hands, feet, elbows, knees, etc.

Wiggle Those Piggies

The whole class will need to remove their shoes and socks for this activity. Point, count, and wiggle each finger and toe while singing "Ten Little Piggies."

Ten Little Piggies
One little, two little, three little piggies,
Four little, five little, six little piggies,
Seven little, eight little, nine little piggies,
Ten little piggy fingers!
(Repeat)
One little, two little, three little piggies,
Four little, five little, six little piggies,
Seven little, eight little, nine little piggies,
Ten little piggy toes!

Extension: Choose a music selection that has a rapid tempo, such as "Flight of the Bumblebee" by Rimsky-Korsakov. Play the music and tell children to move their piggies to the tempo. Instruct students to wiggle their fingers first, then alternate with their toes. Have students wiggle them close together or extend their arms and legs and wiggle their piggies far apart. Let them wiggle their piggies over their heads or down on the floor. Let them wiggle all of their piggies (fingers and toes) on the right side of their bodies, and then on the left. Have them wiggle their piggies behind their backs or in a big circle.

Extension: Play the music again, this time instructing students to let their fingers (or toes) do a little dance on the floor or a tabletop. Tell students to let their fingers and toes kick and bend to the music, shuffle and lilt, or march and stomp. Let students dance their fingers and toes fast, slow, hard, gentle, etc.

ΛΛΛΛΛΛΛΛΛΛΛΛΛΛΛΛΛΛΛΛΛΛΛΛΛΛΛΛΛΛΛΛΛΛΛΛΛΛΛΛΛΛΛΛΛΛΛΛΛΛ

Match and Wiggle . . . .

Using the Body Parts Cards (pages 22–23) (you may
want to enlarge them for easier viewing), have children
match the body part on the card to their own body parts
without verbally identifying them. For example, if you
hold up the hand card, children should wiggle only their
hands to signify that they recognize and can match the
card by their movements. Repeat for other body parts or
hold up more than one card at a time. If you wish, play
music during this activity to add a beat for wiggling.

Circle Sit . . . .

This activity requires a lot of cooperation! Have all of the children stand in a circle, each facing the back of the
child in front of him. Have each child hold on to the waist of the child in front of him. Now, the circle should
squeeze in as tightly as possible so that there are no spaces between children. On your count, tell the group
to simultaneously sit—*very slowly*. If done correctly, the entire circle will sit at once, and each child will be
sitting in the lap of the child behind him. You will probably have a few breaks in the circle before the task is
accomplished, so keep trying!

Body Parts Cards

Activities found on pages 20–21.

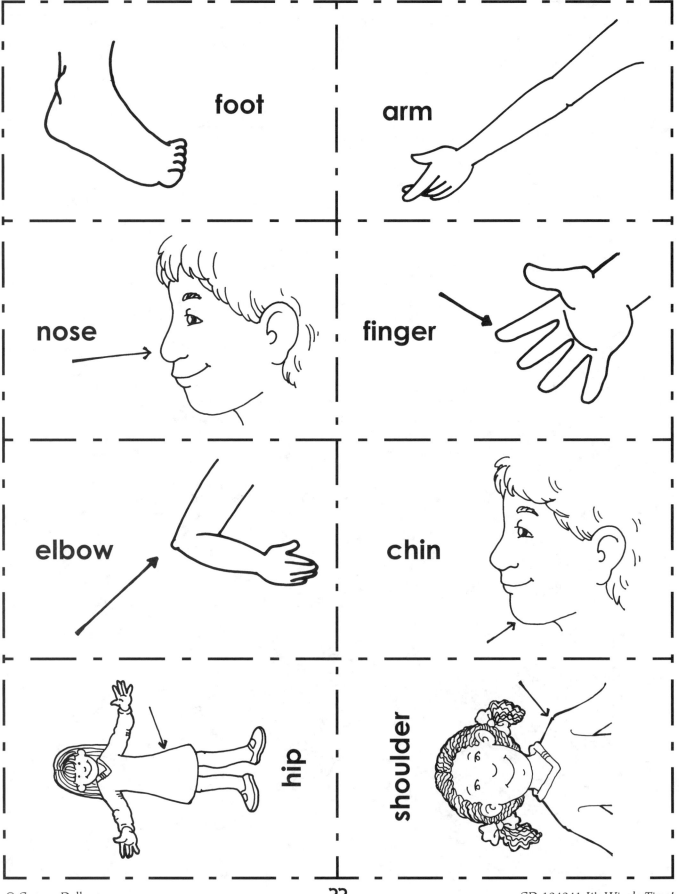

foot

arm

nose

finger

elbow

chin

hip

shoulder

Body Parts Cards

Activities found on pages 20–21.

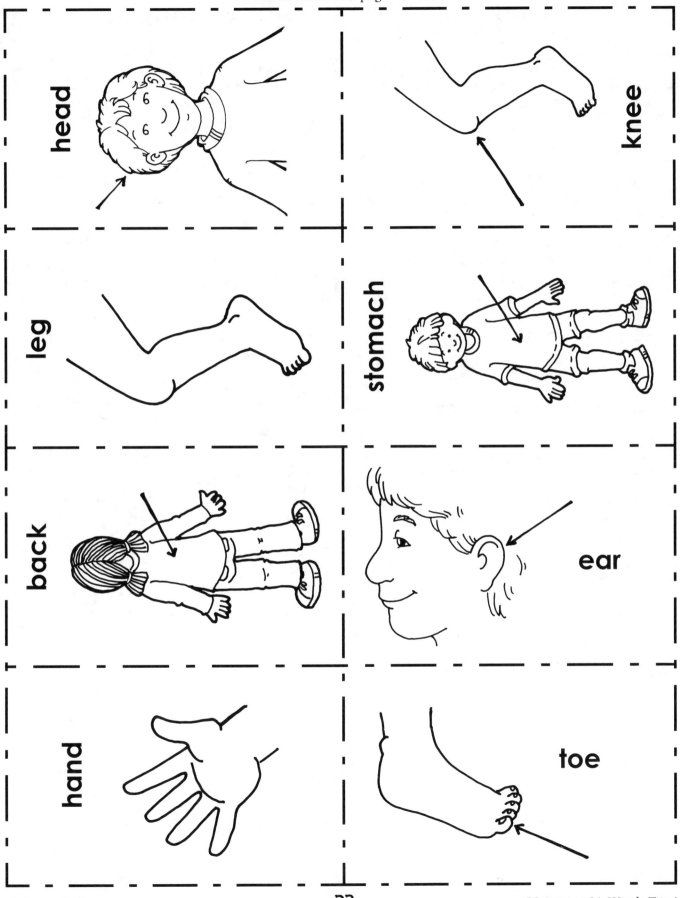

head

knee

leg

stomach

back

ear

hand

toe

Bugs and Other Crawling Things

Butterfly's Life (relaxation story) . . . .

Have each child create his own Insect Headband for this activity using the pattern (page 26). You may want to tape a few sheets of colorful tissue paper to each child's sleeves when he "becomes a butterfly." Play some relaxation music in the background. Use quiet, hushed tones and a soothing voice as you read the following story aloud. Encourage children to move with the story as they listen to the music.

Pretend that you are a caterpillar. You are very hungry. You crawl from one leaf to another by bringing your back end close to your front end with your middle stuck way up in the air. Then, you stretch your front end forward, hungrily munching as you go. Finally, you have eaten so much that you can eat no more. You quietly lie down on a leaf and curl up into a tight ball. Then, you spin a cocoon around yourself and lie very still for a quiet nap.

It is warm and tight inside your cocoon. You try to wiggle and squirm, but your cocoon is so tight that you cannot move your arms and legs. You lie still breathing big, deep breaths. One breath . . . two . . . three . . . and finally you are asleep. You dream of crawling and eating and playing in the sun. You dream of many other things, too.

(Pause for a moment and let children "dream.")

Think about your caterpillar dreams and softly whisper them aloud.

(Quietly encourage each child to whisper as he shares about his caterpillar dreams.)

You rest for a long time, although you are not sure how long you have been asleep. You start to stretch, and suddenly your cocoon begins to pop open! You can hardly wait to get out into the fresh air and sunshine, so you rock back and forth in your cocoon and stretch your arms and legs. You bend forward and backward and up and down until at last you shake the cocoon off of you.

Look! While you were asleep, your body changed from a plump, furry caterpillar to a beautiful butterfly with huge, colorful wings. You gently flap your wings slowly up and then down to dry them in the sun. Up and down, up and down, first very slowly and then faster and faster until suddenly you lift off of your branch and fly into the sunshine. You flit, then float, then flap, and fly through the sky higher and higher than you have ever been.

Below, you see a great field of beautiful flowers. You slowly flutter down and gently land on the biggest and brightest flower in the field. You pump your wings once, twice, and then spread them wide. As you feel the sun on your back, you remember what it was like for you once as a caterpillar, and you do miss the taste of leaves, but you are oh, so happy to be a butterfly.

A Colony of Ants..

Ants work together for the well-being of all of the ants in the mound. Each ant has a specific job, such as gathering food or building bridges. Ants use their sense of smell to follow the scent of the ant in front of them to know where to go to find food.

Collect two or three beanbags for each child. Place the beanbags in a box on one side of the room. Have all of the little "ants" line up single file. You may want children to wear their Insect Headbands (pattern on page 26) for this activity. Remind them that they should follow the path the first little ant travels in order to find lunch. Have the first ant in line crawl quickly across the room, choosing her path as she goes. The rest of the ants should follow closely behind her. When they arrive at the box of beanbags, each ant should grab one, balance it on his back, and continue following the leader back to the mound. The second time, have another ant lead the group, creating a different trail for the others to follow.

Busy Bees...

Like ants, bumblebees are very busy little creatures. They also have a nasty way of defending themselves. If someone bothers a bumblebee, that person is likely to get a little sting. Have one child be the "bumblebee" and wear an Insect Headband (pattern on page 26) to distinguish him from the rest of the crowd. At your signal, have children dart around the play area trying not to get stung by the bumblebee. When the bumblebee catches another player, he tags her, and that child must go sit to the side of the play area to await the next game. The last child standing is the next bumblebee. Continue playing until everyone has had a chance to be the bumblebee. To speed up the game, have two or more children be bumblebees at once.

Spiderweb..

Create your own spiderweb by crisscrossing black yarn back and forth on the floor. Secure the yarn with a piece of tape before changing directions. Ask children to try to go through the spiderweb without touching any of the yarn.

Extension: Make the web maze more challenging by adding another dimension. Instead of making a flat web on the floor, pass the yarn over desks and around chair legs and other obstacles so that children have to crawl over and through the web without getting caught.

Insect Headband Pattern

Activities found on pages 24–25.

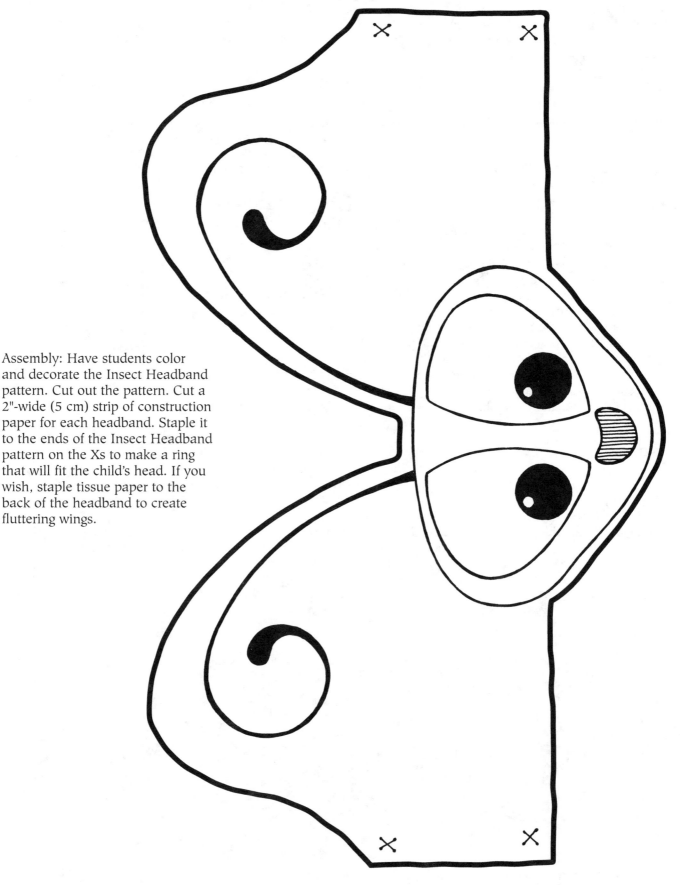

Assembly: Have students color and decorate the Insect Headband pattern. Cut out the pattern. Cut a 2"-wide (5 cm) strip of construction paper for each headband. Staple it to the ends of the Insect Headband pattern on the Xs to make a ring that will fit the child's head. If you wish, staple tissue paper to the back of the headband to create fluttering wings.

CD-104041 *It's Wiggle Time!*

Colors

Frolicking Rainbows . . . .
Cut crepe paper streamers in red, orange, yellow, green, blue, and purple for each child. Stack the streamers in order and staple together. Cut out wristbands for each child using a strip of colorful construction paper or card stock. Secure the streamers to the wristbands and staple the bands in loops.

Play music and let students dance with the streamers to create frolicking rainbows. Encourage children to "paint the sky" with the streamers by moving their arms in big circles. Let children continue dancing and painting until they are certain they have covered the entire room in rainbows.

Variation: Attach the streamers to craft sticks instead of wristbands.

Yarn Path . . . .
Create a pattern all over the floor with one strand of colorful yarn, securing it to the floor with tape. Repeat with a second color. Keep each color in a repeating pattern. For instance, place yellow yarn in a big swirl, hot pink yarn in long straight rows, red yarn in zigzags, etc. The colors may cross over each other.

Cut a paper medallion to match each yarn color. Punch a hole in the medallion and create a necklace using the matching yarn. Give each child a necklace to remind her which path to follow. Let each child have a turn following all of the paths.

Variation: Play music to encourage different walking styles. For example, have children walk heel-toe on one path, do the bear crawl (hands and feet on the floor) on another, walk backward on a third, tiptoe on a fourth, etc. When children have made their way through each path, have them go in reverse.

Switched-Up Twist-Up . . . .

Obtain four, colorful dot stickers (red, yellow, green, and blue) for each child. Have each student place a red sticker on her left hand, a yellow sticker on her right hand, a green sticker on her left foot, and a blue sticker on her right foot. Create two, two-sided flags to use as signals. Cut out four construction paper rectangles, one in each color. Glue the red rectangle to the yellow rectangle with a craft-stick handle in the middle. Do the same with the blue and green rectangles.

Use the colorful flags to signal which limb children should hold up in the air. For example, show them the yellow flag, and they should hold up their right hands. Repeat with the other three colors to make sure that everyone knows which hand or foot to move when you show the corresponding flag. Flash the color flags more and more quickly while children try to match your signals. See how long it takes for them to get really twisted up!

Extension: Repeat the activity using other body parts, such as the head, knees, hips, etc. Give a wiggle command, such as "shake," and children will match body parts and actions.

Color Mixing (movement rhyme)

Have students sing or chant the rhyme while following the directions for each color.

Color Mixing

Red makes my feet tap,   *(tap feet)*
And yellow makes my hands clap.   *(clap hands)*
But when I mix red and yellow,
I get a tappin', clappin' ORANGE!   *(tap and clap together)*

Yellow makes my head shake,   *(shake head)*
And blue makes my knees quake,   *(make knees quiver)*
But when I mix yellow and blue,
I get a shakin', quakin' GREEN!   *(shake and quiver together)*

Blue makes my hips wiggle,   *(wiggle hips)*
And red makes my shoulders jiggle.   *(jiggle shoulders)*
But when I mix blue and red,
I get a wigglin', jigglin' PURPLE!   *(wiggle and jiggle together)*

Mixing colors is so much fun,
I could do purple, orange, and green   *(do all of the actions together)*
Until the day is done!

Sock Score

You will need a variety of pairs of colorful socks for this activity. Three or four different colors should be plenty. Ask parents for donations of mismatched socks or dye white socks if necessary.

Divide the class into teams. You will need as many teams as you have sock colors. Place the socks in a big box or bin on one side of the room. Tape a starting line on the other side of the room. Have children take off their shoes and socks and line up with their teams at the starting line. Give each team a color to search for in the sock bin. Players on the blue team will retrieve only blue socks, the yellow team retrieves only yellow socks, etc. At your signal, have the first player on each team dash (or crawl, or skip, or hop, etc.) to the other side of the room, retrieve one sock that matches the team color, put it on her foot, and race back to the starting line.

Then, the next player in line runs to the box in search of another matching sock. Continue playing for a specified time. When time is up, count the total number of socks each team retrieved. Write *blue*, *yellow*, and *red* (or whatever colors you may be using) on the board and keep a tally of the total number of socks each team retrieved. Repeat, giving each team a new sock color. At the end of the game, see which color has the highest score!

Variation: Let each child choose which color he wants to retrieve in the relay. At the end of the game, tally the total for each color to see which one was the most popular. If you wish, create a bar graph to document your findings.

Extension: For a real challenge, practice color mixing using the socks. For example, give a student a blue sock and tell him to retrieve the sock that he needs to make green (a yellow sock), etc.

Community Helpers

Dr. Untangle

Divide the class into teams of five or six children. Have one child on each team be "Dr. Untangle" and hide his eyes or leave the room for a few minutes. The remaining children on each team join hands in a circle, facing the middle. Without letting go of each other's hands, children should tangle themselves up by twisting and turning, crawling over or under arms, etc.

When they are sufficiently knotted, they should call the doctor to help them get untangled. The trick is that the circle cannot be broken to untangle the knot, so Dr. Untangle must undo children's twisting without taking them apart. If he is successful, the circle will be completely intact when they are untwisted.

Variation: This activity can be done with one giant class circle, but it takes a lot of patience to untangle such a knot!

Bucket Brigade

This is a fun outdoor activity for field day. Instruct children to hold hands standing in a circle, facing the middle. Tell them all to take one big step backward and let go of their classmates' hands. There should now be some space between all of the children. Widen the gap between two of the children and place a full bucket of water next to one of them and an empty bucket next to the other one. Place three or four large plastic cups by the child with the full bucket. This child should fill the first cup by dipping it into the bucket of water and then pass the cup to the next child in the circle. This child should then pass the cup of water on to the next child and on and on around the circle. A second cup may be started after the first cup has made it halfway around the circle. The last child in the circle should pour the water into the empty bucket and set the cup next to the child who is filling cups from the bucket. See how quickly they can pass the water without spilling it. If you wish, set a goal by drawing a fill line on the empty bucket.

Variation: Use several large sponges instead of cups for passing the water. Have the first student soak them in the bucket and pass them around the circle. The last student should wring the sponges into the empty bucket.

Stop and Go

Choose one child to be the police officer who directs traffic. Let all of the other children move and dance freely until the officer yells, "Stop!," at which point everyone should freeze. When the officer yells, "Go!," children should continue their free movement. If desired, play some music in the background to inspire the dancers.

Variation: Mark a starting line on one side of the play area and have children stand on the line. Choose one child to be the police officer. Have her wear a police hat, if desired, and have her stand with her back to the group on the opposite side of the play area. When the officer says, "Green light!," have children move as quickly and quietly as possible toward the police officer until she yells, "Red light!" At this command, children must freeze. As the police officer yells this, she should spin around and try to catch children before they are able to freeze. If she catches anyone who is still moving, that child must return to the starting line and begin again. The first child to reach the officer becomes the next police officer.

ΛΛΛΛΛΛΛΛΛΛΛΛΛΛΛΛΛΛΛΛΛΛΛΛΛΛΛΛΛΛΛΛΛΛΛΛΛΛΛΛΛΛΛΛ

Special Delivery

On several slips of paper (one for each child in the class), write actions or activities, such as "Jump up and down 10 times" or "Do the crab walk across the room and back." Seal each slip of paper in an envelope. Write each child's name on an envelope. Obtain a large mailbox or create one with a shoe box. Sing the following rhyme to the tune of "Twinkle, Twinkle Little Star."

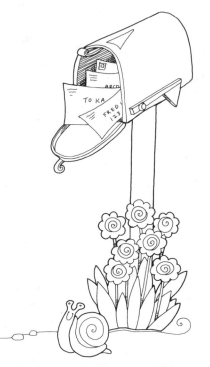

> **Special Delivery**
> What is in the mail today?
> Open the door, and then we'll play.
> Is it a note or a bill?
> Whatever it is, we'll love it still.
> What is in the mail today?
> Open the door, and then we'll play.

Open the mailbox and select an envelope. Have the child whose name is written on the envelope claim his letter. When he opens his mail, help him read the instructions and have him lead the class in the suggested activity.

Variation: Place 10 pictures of mailboxes around the room. Write a number, 1 through 10, on the side of each mailbox and tape a sealed activity suggestion (see ideas above) to the back side of each mailbox picture. Have one child select a number (1 through 10) at random and go to the corresponding mailbox. Have her return with the "mail" and deliver it to you. Open the envelope and let her lead the class in the suggested activity.

Dentist

Lead students in singing or chanting while they pretend to brush and floss their teeth.

> **Brushing and Flossing**
> Brush, brush, brush, brush, brush, brush. *(move hands up and down as if using a toothbrush)*
> The brush goes round and round.
> Floss, floss, floss, floss, floss, floss.   *(move hands up and down as if using a piece of floss)*
> The floss goes up and down.
> When I brush and floss my teeth,
> My dentist will always say,
> "I like to see those pearly whites,
> Here's a sticker for you today!"

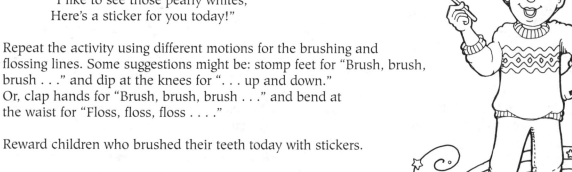

Repeat the activity using different motions for the brushing and flossing lines. Some suggestions might be: stomp feet for "Brush, brush, brush . . ." and dip at the knees for ". . . up and down." Or, clap hands for "Brush, brush, brush . . ." and bend at the waist for "Floss, floss, floss . . . ."

Reward children who brushed their teeth today with stickers.

ΛΛΛΛΛΛΛΛΛΛΛΛΛΛΛΛΛΛΛΛΛΛΛΛΛΛΛΛΛΛΛΛΛΛΛΛΛΛΛΛΛΛΛΛ

Emotions

Emotional Walk

Faces and body language often tell stories about how people feel. They can tell others about how someone feels or give hints about the kind of day that person is having. Let students sing or chant the following lines to the beat of "Here We Go 'Round the Mulberry Bush." Have students show the emotions using facial expressions and body language.

Emotional Walk

This is the way a happy person walks—
Romp! Romp, romp! Romp, romp! Romp!   *(boisterously skip around with a big grin)*
This is the way a mad person walks—
Stomp! Stomp, stomp! Stomp, stomp! Stomp!   *(clench fists at sides and stomp with a furrowed brow)*
This is the way a scared person walks—
Tiptoe. Tiptoe. Tiptoe.   *(tiptoe gingerly with a frightened expression)*
This is the way a tired person walks—
Slow. Slow, slow. Slow, slow. Slow.   *(slide feet sluggishly and yawn with droopy eyes)*
This is the way a sad person walks—
Slump. Slump, slump. Slump, slump. Slump.   *(drop shoulders and drag feet with a forlorn expression)*
This is the way a cranky person walks—
Grump! Grump, grump! Grump, grump! Grump!   *(fold arms and stomp around with a frustrated look)*

Create other emotions and actions for the rhyme.

Wave the Blues Away

Draw a reversible sad/happy face on six to eight blue balloons or beach balls. (See illustration at the right.) Explain that feeling sad is sometimes called "the blues." Show a sad balloon face and explain that sometimes the music we listen to sounds sad or blue, too. Play a selection of blues or melancholy music, such as "I Feel Like Goin' Home" by Muddy Waters (*Muddy Waters, His Best: 1947-1955*, MCA, 1997) or "Blues with B. B." by B. B. King (*Spotlight on Lucille*, Virgin Records, 1992). Now, rotate the balloon upside down to reveal a happy, smiling face. Remind children that when a person feels blue, he can do things to turn the frown upside down and feel happy again.

Using a parachute or a large blanket, have each child grab a parachute handle or an edge of the blanket. Toss the balloons on top of the parachute. Play the blues music again and have children gently toss the balloons by undulating the parachute up and down. Vary the movements of the parachute by making small shallow waves and then big deep waves. See how long it takes to shake all of the blue balloon faces onto the floor. When the blues are gone and everyone is smiling again, change to a more upbeat music selection and continue to experiment with how the balloons move as the parachute wiggles and waves.

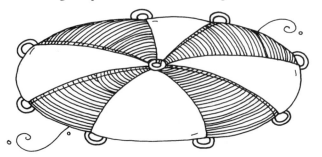

Variation: For a coordination challenge, try using heavier items like soft foam balls, beanbags, etc., instead of balloons or beach balls. They will fly higher and faster when the parachute moves.

Food

Making Breakfast . . . .

Making breakfast can be a lot of fun for you and the children—especially when they get to "cook" with their whole bodies and nobody has to clean up the kitchen when you are done! Try these creative activities to make breakfast in the classroom. During each activity, you should act like the chef, calling out and mimicking the instructions like the host of a television cooking show.

Scrambled Eggs: Instruct children to become "eggs" by crouching into tight balls on the floor. Now, the eggs should get ready to "crack" open by rolling around, still curled tightly in balls. When you call out "Scrambled eggs!," the eggs should crack open, jump up, and swirl around like eggs being whisked in a bowl. You should act like a chef stirring the giant mix. When the eggs are sufficiently scrambled, pour them into a giant imaginary classroom frying pan and have them mix around as you cook them and stir them with a big imaginary spatula.

Sizzling Bacon: Tell all of the "bacon" to lie flat on the ground stretched out as far as they can with their arms extended above their heads. Tell them that you are "turning up the heat" in the imaginary frying pan, so the bacon should start to sizzle. As it gets hotter and hotter, the bacon should make sizzling sounds and wiggle all over! Use your big imaginary spatula to flip the bacon over when it is time to cook the other side.

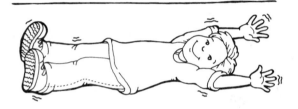

Fresh Squeezed Juice: Squeezing orange juice is tough work for the arm muscles, even when it is imaginary. You will need all of the classroom chefs to help you. Have each chef pretend to cut some oranges in half. It will take several "oranges," so be sure to "cut" plenty. Now, have everyone take one orange half and "squeeze" it by pressing his hands together and rotating them in opposite directions. See if children can squeeze 20 oranges—squeeze and count together!

Flip the Pancakes: In this activity, each child will become a pancake. First, you need to stir your "batter." Have children rotate in a small circle to make sure they are thoroughly "mixed." Now, "pour" the batter into your giant imaginary frying pan by having them gently drop into balls on the floor. As the batter spreads out, children should spread their arms and legs out as widely as possible. After the pancakes "cook" on one side for a little while, take your big imaginary spatula and help them flip over to finish cooking on the other side. See how creative the "pancakes" can be when they try to flip over with their arms and legs extended—it would be a shame to lose the shape of those big pancakes! When this "batch" is finished, start over so that there will be a big stack of pancakes for breakfast.

Hot Potato

Have children sit in a circle, facing the middle. Give one child a large baking potato. (A beanbag works well, too.) Choose one child to be the chef and have him sit in the middle of the circle. The chef should hide his eyes while the other children pass the potato as quickly and quietly as they can. (It is a hot potato, after all!) At any point, the chef may call out, "Hot potato!" Whoever is holding the potato at that moment is "thrown into the pot" (the middle of the circle) for "cooking," and play continues until only one student has not been thrown in the pot. The last child will get to be the chef for the next round.

Variation: Play the game to music. Instead of having the chef only call out, "Hot potato!," have him start and stop the music, as well.

Fruit Basket Turnover

Divide the class into three groups—bananas, apples, and oranges. Have children sit in chairs in a circle, facing the middle. Choose one child to be the farmer and stand in the middle of the circle. Remove her chair so that there will always be one child without a seat. Have the farmer call out a fruit group, for example, "bananas." At this time, the banana group should jump up and exchange seats, trying to get a different seat in the circle before the farmer takes one. The child who is left without a seat now becomes the farmer and calls out another fruit name. An alternative is for the farmer to occasionally to call out, "Fruit basket turnover!" When this happens, everyone in the class should jump up and hurry to find a new seat. Repeat the game using various fruits as group names.

Friends

Push Me, Pull Me

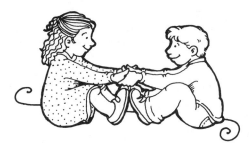

Have each child choose a friend or partner. You will need a variety of music samples with different tempos. Play the first sample while clapping to the beat. When students are accustomed to the beat, give them the following directions:

Sit toe-to-toe with knees bent. Clasp your hands. Being sure to keep your bottoms on the floor, one friend should gently pull the other's arms toward him, causing her to bend forward at the waist. The other friend should then repeat the action, pulling her partner toward her. Repeat the rocking action while keeping time to the music.

Now, switch to music that has a different beat and repeat the activity.

Variations: Have students try: standing facing each other and clasping hands; sitting back-to-back and linking elbows; standing back-to-back and linking elbows; lying on the floor touching feet with legs bent in the "bicycle" position; etc. See how many "Push Me, Pull Me" combinations children can make.

Hello Friend

This is an excellent activity for beginning the day. Sometimes people like to say "hello" using their voices, and sometimes they use their bodies. Have children echo your voice and actions.

Invite everyone to sit in a circle with you. Sing "Hello _____," inserting a child's name. Have children repeat the greeting by echoing your voice. Also, try using different voices and accents, such as a western twang, a southern belle, a scary monster, etc. The child whose name is called should stand up and choose an action to greet each child around the circle. He might choose a hug, a handshake, a high five, a two-arm wave, etc. Each child in the group should repeat the action as she is greeted by the chosen child. Repeat the activity using synonym phrases for "hello," such as, "greetings" or "salutations," or choose greetings in different languages. More language suggestions and sound clips are available on the Internet.

Language	Hello
French:	Bonjour (bohn•ZHOOR)
German:	Guten tag (GOOT•en tahk)
Hawaiian:	Aloha (ah•LOH•hah)
Hebrew:	Shalom (sha•LOHM)
Italian:	Buon giorno (bwohn JOR•noh)
Japanese:	Konichiwa (koh•NEE•chee•wah)
Mandarin Chinese:	Ni hao (nee haOW)
Spanish:	Hola (OH•lah)

Escort

Set up a simple obstacle course using cones, boxes, ropes, tubes, etc., or designate a path through the playground equipment. Write each child's name on a piece of paper and place it in a bowl. Draw two names from the bowl. Have one child close his eyes while the second child takes him by the hand and carefully leads him through the obstacle course. Have the escorts give verbal instructions to their partners, such as "duck," "step up," "turn to your right," etc., to help them move through the course. Remind students to trust their friends to lead them safely. Repeat, having children change positions so that each gets to have a turn as the escort.

Crazy Handshake

Everyone needs a partner for this action rhyme. As students say the chant, have them shake hands, Then, have them simultaneously shake each body part as it is mentioned. End with big shaky hugs!

Crazy Handshake
When I greet some friends of mine,
I always shake their hands.
But a funny thing starts happening,
Something we never planned.

The shake moves past our hands,
And travels up our arms,
Then to our hips, and legs, and feet,
We hope there's no serious harm.

For as the shake spreads to the neck and the head,
And over the back so slow,
We discover the best way to greet friends we meet,
Is to shake with them from our heads down to our toes!

Lean on Me

Divide children so that each child has a partner. Friends always help each other and offer lots of support. Adults often call this "leaning on each other." Have students practice listening and balancing skills by actually leaning on their friends as directed. First, they should stand facing each other. Then, they should put both hands out so that they are touching their partners' palms. Instruct them to gently put their weight on their hands and lean into their partners simultaneously. Now, they will be supporting each other with their hands!

Variation: When this is mastered (without too many spills), try having students raise one leg and then the other while leaning. Or, tell them to try to lean against each other, back-to-back, and lower themselves to the ground. See which team is the most "supportive!"

Holidays

Drop-and-Run Valentines. . . . .

The object of this game is to see if students can deliver secret valentines without getting caught. Every child needs a Valentine Envelope pattern (page 37) with her name written as the return address. Now, select one child to be the "Valentine." Have him sit on the floor on one side of the play area with his back to the class. Mark a starting line on the opposite side of the area. Taking turns so that only one child is moving at once, have children cross the play area as quietly as possible. The object is to try to deliver the envelope by placing it on the floor behind the Valentine and then run back to the starting point. If the Valentine hears the deliverer, he should try to tag her before she gets back to the starting line.

Let students experiment with different ways to get across the room quietly, such as tiptoeing, crawling, creeping slowly, etc., or let them go for it and hope to outrun the Valentine. If a child has an unsuccessful delivery and gets caught, she becomes the next Valentine.

St. Patrick's Day Pot of Gold Hunt . . . .

Help each child make his own leprechaun hat to wear for this activity using the pattern (page 38). You will need one, too!

Laminate several sheets of gold paper. Make lots of gold coins by cutting 2" (5 cm) circles. With a permanent marker, write the numbers 1 through 5 on the coins so that each coin has one number written on it. Hide the coins, number-side down, around the room. Have children sit close to you. Tell them that you are a lucky leprechaun who has hidden your gold coins for good little boys and girls. Each child should then raise his hand and ask the Lucky Leprechaun for permission to look for a coin by saying, "Lucky Leprechaun, may I go hunt for gold?" Respond by acknowledging his wish, but explain that he must follow your directions. For example, you might say, "Yes, but you must take baby steps." The child should then baby step around the room until he finds a coin. Then, he should return to the circle to await his next turn.

When all of the children have taken turns finding gold coins, play again using the numbers on the coins that they found during the first round. This time, when a child is acknowledged, has asked politely, and has been given a movement challenge, she should try to find the number of coins indicated on the first coin she found. For example, if the child's first coin has the number 5 on it, she should try to find five coins on her second turn.

Valentine Envelope Pattern

Activity found on page 36.

To: My Valentine Friend

From:

Leprechaun Hat Pattern

Activity found on page 36.

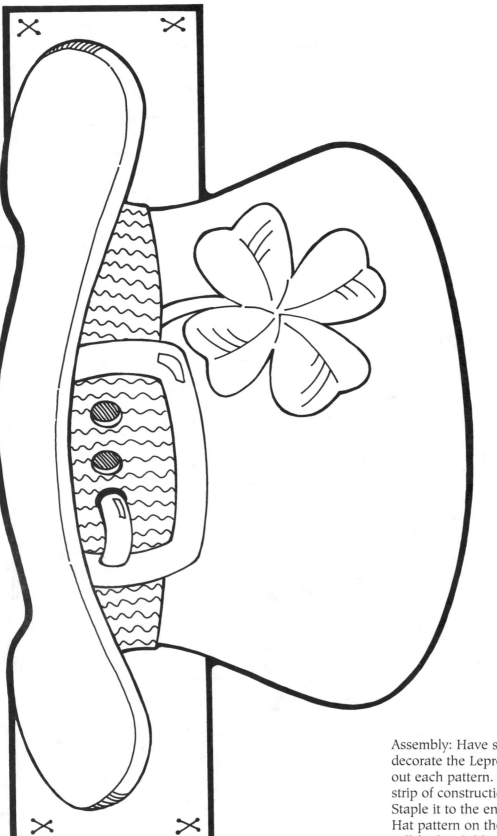

Assembly: Have students color and decorate the Leprechaun Hat pattern. Cut out each pattern. Cut a 2"-wide (5 cm) strip of construction paper for each hat. Staple it to the ends of the Leprechaun Hat pattern on the Xs to make a ring that will fit the child's head.

Trick-or-Treat Halloween . . . .

Make two sets of cards with jack-o'-lantern faces on them. On one set, draw smiling faces; on the other set, draw frowning faces. Make sure there are enough for each child in the class to have one card. Have the class sit in a circle, facing the middle. Spread the circle as widely as possible. Give each child a card, but turn it facedown so that no one can see the pumpkin face.

Choose one child to go trick-or-treating. While the class sings the trick-or-treat song below, this child should skip around the inside of the circle. When the song stops, the trick-or-treater should stop in front of one child in the circle. The sitting child should ask, "Trick or treat?" The trick-or-treater must guess if his classmate has a trick card (frowning jack-o'-lantern) or a treat card (smiling jack-o'-lantern). If he guesses correctly, he should continue skipping around the classroom to the trick-or-treat song. If he guesses incorrectly, he must do a trick of his choice, such as hopping on one foot or leaping like a frog, and trade places with the other child, who then begins her turn.

Trick-or-Treat Song
(Sing to the tune of "Row, Row, Row Your Boat.")

Halloween is coming, the pumpkin's getting big.
Is it a trick, or is it a treat? Let's dance a little jig!

Variation: Write appropriate "tricks" ("Do 10 jumping jacks," "Act like an elephant," "Make a funny face," etc.) on cards and place them in a bowl. Have students draw from this bowl whenever they need to perform tricks. Also, have the entire class stand up and join the trick-or-treaters in performing the trick activities.

Hanukkah Dreidel . . . .

Children play with the dreidel, a top-like toy, when celebrating the Jewish holiday of Hanukkah. The dreidel has four sides. Each side has a Hebrew character printed on it. Depending on which side is showing when the dreidel stops spinning, the spinner is supposed to perform certain activities.

Make a dreidel by covering a square box with paper. Print the four Hebrew characters *Nun*, *Gimmel*, *Hey*, and *Shin*, one on each side of the box. Print "roll again" on the top and bottom of the box. Have children sit in a large circle.

Begin by having one child roll the "dreidel die." In the real dreidel game, a certain number of tokens are traded for each Hebrew character. For the purpose of this game, the actions for the four Hebrew characters will be:

Nun: The girls walk the circle.
Gimmel: The boys walk the circle.
Hey: The girls walk the circle backward.
Shin: The boys walk the circle backward.

ש ה ג נ

Nun   Gimmel   Hey   Shin

For instance, assume that a *Nun* is rolled. All of the girls should find spots around the outside of the circle and skip back to where they started while the class sings the dreidel song. Try creating different actions for each Hebrew character.

I Have a Little Dreidel
(Sing to the tune of "Dreidel, Dreidel, Dreidel.")

I have a little dreidel,
I love to make it spin,
And when it stops its spinning,
It drops, and then we win!

Christmas Reindeer Games . . . .

According to the famous song about Rudolph, Santa's reindeer love to play reindeer games. Try these fun games to get the "reindeer" ready for the big day.

Hook Horns: You will need a small hoop for each team. Use a small plastic hoop or create one by rolling a sheet of newspaper on the diagonal and taping the ends together in a loop. Divide the class into pairs. Give each team of "reindeer" their own hoop. Tell them that their arms are their antlers. As one team member tosses the hoop, the other team member should try to catch it on one of her "antlers." Now, have players switch roles.

Santa's Sleigh: A big part of preparing for Christmas is loading Santa's sleigh. Divide the class into small teams. Place a large box at one end of the room to represent Santa's sleigh and mark a starting line on the opposite side of the room. Load an assortment of toys from the room into a large garbage bag for each team. Make sure there is an equal number of toys in each bag. Set these bags on the starting line across from the large box. At your signal, the first player on each team should grab one toy out of his team bag and race to place it in the "sleigh" on the opposite side of the room. The player should race back to the starting line and tag the next reindeer in line. Continue the relay until the sleigh is full and the toy bags are empty. For a challenge, have students fill the sleigh by skipping, crawling, crab walking, etc., instead of running.

Leaping Lessons: Practice leaping skills! Mark a starting line with a piece of tape. Have the little "reindeer" in the class line up behind the line. Have them take turns standing on the line and leaping forward to see who can leap the farthest. Line up again and see who can beat his first try.

Now, place several obstacles, such as blocks or small storage boxes, around the room and have the reindeer leap through the obstacle course.

Ring in a Happy New Year. . . . .

Ring in the New Year with a bell-ringing bonanza. String three or four small jingle bells onto a chenille craft stick. Make four chenille-bell sticks for each child. Depending on children's developmental levels, you may want to use only one or two chenille-bell sticks for each child. Loosely twist the chenille sticks onto each child's ankles and wrists. Have them practice jingling the bells loudly, softly, quickly, and slowly. Let them jingle on their right sides and then on their left sides. Have them jingle with their hands over their heads, straight out to their sides, and behind their backs. Now, let them jingle just their feet, first one and then the other. See if children can move their bodies without making *any* jingle bell noises. Or, see if they can walk all the way across the room without making jingle bell noises.

Extension: Count down to the New Year! Have children crouch down into tight balls. Count down from 10 together. At the end of the countdown, have children jump up, dancing and waving and making as much bell noise as possible. At your signal, have children freeze and crouch down again for another countdown.

Numbers

Body Math (finger play) ....

Have students take off their shoes and socks for this fun chant.

Body Math

I have 10 fingers,	(hold up and wiggle fingers)
I have 10 toes,	(wiggle toes)
I have two legs,	(wiggle legs)
And that's how it goes.	
I have two eyes,	(point to eyes and blink)
Two ears, lips, and hands,	(point to ears and lips, then clap)
I have two feet	
For marching in bands.	(march in place)
I have one head,	(wiggle head)
And one back you see,	(put hands on back)
Because all of these numbers	
Add up to me!	(jump and spread arms over head)

Shake, Clap, Count ....

Gather 10 large wooden beads, milk container caps, or other similar-sized manipulatives. Write one number on each bead, 1 through 10. Place all of the beads in a large container with a lid. Select one child to come to the front of the group. Have the child shake the container vigorously. Tell her to open the lid, reach inside without looking, and remove one bead. Have her read the number and lead the class in clapping that many times. Next, have her choose a movement activity for the class. For instance, if the number 3 bead is drawn, she could choose to do three jumping jacks. Continue playing until everyone has the opportunity to draw a bead.

Extension: Have children select two beads at once and add the numbers together. For example, if a number 2 and a number 7 are drawn, the class would do the movement activity a total of 9 times.

Musical Number March ....

Prepare numbered manipulatives as directed in the "Shake, Clap, Count" activity (above). Prepare an 11th bead with a star on it. Using index cards, create number cards with the numbers 1 through 10. Make additional cards with stars on them so that there are enough cards for each child. For instance, if there are 25 students in the class, you would need number cards 1 through 10 and 15 cards with stars on them. Laminate the cards for durability. Randomly tape the cards in a circle on the floor, number- or star-side up.

Play a music selection while children march around the circle of cards. When the music stops, each child should stop on the card closest to him. Make sure that everyone has a card. Draw a bead from the container. If it is a numbered bead, have the child who is standing on the card with that number lead the group in an activity of his choice (touching toes, for example) the number of times indicated. If the star bead is chosen, everyone standing on a star card must quickly find a new star card by switching with a child who is also standing on a star card.

Extension: For an additional challenge, add higher numbers or duplicate the number cards and have children perform the movement challenges with partners.

Number Pass

Obtain enough construction paper for each child to have one piece. Number these papers sequentially up to the total number of children in the class. (For example, if there are eight students in the class, number the papers 1 through 8.) Laminate for durability. Tape or safety pin the papers to the fronts of children's shirts so that everyone can see them.

Have children stand in random order in a circle, facing the middle. Give the child wearing the number 1 a ball. Instruct her to toss it to the child who is wearing the number 2. Have students continue tossing the ball sequentially until everyone has caught it. The last child in the sequence should toss the ball back to the child wearing the number 1.

Shuffle children and start over, or have them exchange the numbers they are wearing for new numbers. For an added challenge, begin a second ball after the first ball is about halfway through the numbers.

Variation: Have children sit down in the circle and roll the ball to each other instead of tossing it.

Number Path

Using different colors of tape or yarn, create four zigzag patterns across the room. (If you use yarn, secure it to the floor as you change directions.) Make sure that there are nine angles in each zigzag pattern. The patterns can cross each other, if desired. Make four sets of 10 number cards, labeled 1 through 10. Tape the number 1s at the beginning of each path. Tape the other numbers in succession at the angles in the zigzag patterns, placing the number 10s at the ends of the paths. Beginning with the number 1, have children jump from number to number on their chosen paths and count aloud as they go. Tell them to try to step, jump, or land only on the numbers, not along the paths. Next, have them choose second paths and hop from number to number. Try a third time having them use giant steps to move backward. On the fourth try, have them move caterpillar-style so that the hands reach the numbers first and then the back ends inch up to join the front ends.

Extension: Mix up the numbers along the paths and have children find and jump to each of the numbers in sequential order.

I Can Move 100 Ways!

When celebrating the 100th day of school, have the class help you make a list of 100 ways they can move their bodies. This may include simple actions, such as bending a finger, or whole body actions, such as doing a somersault. When the list is complete, try to do all of the actions in order as a class. Make sure that number 100 is "Lie down for a rest!"

On the Farm

Old MacDonald's Barnyard Opera

Create your own barnyard opera while singing "Old MacDonald Had a Farm." Enlarge the Farm Animal Cards (page 45). Color the cards as desired and laminate for durability. Hold up the picture of each animal while singing about it. Each time children sing the animal noises, have them perform the corresponding actions. For instance, while singing about the cow, they should wiggle their "tails" whenever they say "Moo." Continue the song, having students add a different animal and a different action to the sequence each time. Be sure to have students use loud, operatic voices when singing "E-I-E-I-O!"

Old MacDonald Had a Farm
Old MacDonald had a farm,
E-I-E-I-O!
And on this farm he had a *cow*,
E-I-E-I-O!
With a *Moo, Moo* here, and a *Moo, Moo* there,
Here a *Moo*, there a *Moo*, everywhere a *Moo, Moo*.
Old MacDonald had a farm,
E-I-E-I-O!

Cow: "Moo" and wiggle the "tail."
Horse: "Neigh" and shake the "mane."
Sheep: "Baa" and alternate quickly stomping the feet.
Pig: "Oink" and "root" in the "mud."
Cat: "Meow" and wipe a "paw" on the face.
Goose: "Honk," extend the neck, and "flap" the "wings."
Dog: "Bark" and bound around.
Goat: "Bleat" and scratch the ground with a "hoof."
Chicken: "Cluck" and strut around the room.

Variation: Have children sing using musical styles besides opera, such as blues, rap, country, or rock and roll.

Bringin' in the Hay

You will need *many, many* 1" (2½ cm) strips of newspaper for this activity. The horses are hungry, and the cows want to eat. It is the farmer's job to make sure the livestock have plenty of hay. Put the "farmhands" to work filling the "barn" with "hay." Write the numbers 1 to 10 on separate sheets of paper. Scatter the strips of newspaper in the "field." Have all of the farmhands line up. One at a time, show each child a piece of paper with a number on it. The child should run to the field and collect that number of pieces of hay. For instance, if you show the first child the number 5, she should retrieve 5 pieces of hay. Have children move as quickly as possible. Continue bringin' in the hay—each time with a new challenge, such as, "Jump over the mud puddles on your way across the field," "Hop on one foot," "Tiptoe quietly so that you do not wake the rooster," etc.— until all of the hay is in the barn. For an added challenge, use simple math sentences instead of numbers for hay gathering.

Extension: Bring an outdoor activity indoors! Load all of the hay into a wagon and let children take turns having "tractor" rides around the "barnyard."

Who Is in the Barn? . . . .

Make a copy of the Farm Animal Cards (page 45). Color as desired and laminate for durability. Choose one child to be the farmer and have him wait in the hallway. Choose a second child to hide in the "barn" (in a closet, under your desk, behind a curtain, etc.). Have the second child select an animal card. When the "farmer" returns to the room, have him ask, "Who is in the barn?" The child who is hiding should reply by making the sound of the animal she chose. For example, if the child chose the cow card, she would reply by saying, "Moooo!" The farmer must now guess which animal is in the barn and which classmate is imitating that animal.

Variation: Play "Who Is in the Hay?" using the pile of newspaper from the "Bringin' in the Hay" activity (page 43). Instead of hiding in a closet or under your desk, have the child hide under the pile of "hay" and jump out to reveal herself after the farmer tries to guess her identity.

Barn Dance . . . .

Everyone needs a bandana for this activity. Have each child put the bandana in his back pocket or tuck it in the waistband of his pants. Play a square-dancing song or a folk song, such as "Cotton-Eyed Joe" by Kimbo (*All-Time Favorite Dances*, Kimbo Records, 1998), and have a barn dance. Begin with everyone standing in a circle, hands on hips, bouncing at the knees to the beat. Have students hold hands and shuffle to the left and then to the right. The group should skip to the middle (still holding hands), throw their hands in the air, shout "Yee-haw!," and move back to the circle. Now, everyone should take a partner by the elbow and wave his bandana in the air while turning in circles one way and then the other. Let students continue dancing, adding in other square-dancing moves (such as do-si-do, etc.), clapping, stomping, and shouting, "Yee-haw!" until the music stops.

Mixed-Up Barnyard . . . .

Make enough copies of the Farm Animal Cards (page 45) for each child to have one card. Tell children that the only sounds they can make are the sounds of the animals on their cards. For instance, children who draw goose cards can only say, "honk, honk." Explain that the object of the activity is to wander around and find all of the matching animals by listening for the correct sound. Remind children that they cannot make any sounds other than their animal sounds. If there are more than two children with each type of animal card, encourage them to hold hands and stick together until they find the other matching animals.

Galloping Horses . . . .

Each child will need two paper cups. Show them how to gently tap the cups on the table or tap them together to make a clapping-hooves sound. When you say "Giddyap!," the "horses" should begin clopping along. When you say "Whoa!," the horses should stop and freeze. Let students prance and gallop around the play area while making hoof sounds. Tell them to throw in a few "neighs" and "whinnies," too!

Extension: Create a steeplechase course of obstacles for the horses to jump over or ride around while making hoof sounds.

Farm Animal Cards

Activities found on pages 43–44.

cow

horse

goose

chicken

sheep

goat

dog

cat

pig

Opposites

Opposite Me

Tell children that no matter what you do, you want them to do the opposite. Discuss the concept of opposites if necessary. Perform several different activities and see if children can come up with opposite actions. Do not give them any suggestions; let them explore for a few seconds until everyone is satisfied that he is doing the opposite of what you are doing. Then, move on to the next movement. Here are some suggested activities: stand tall with arms straight in the air, run in place very slowly, hop on one foot, spin in a circle, bend over and touch your toes, wiggle very fast, etc. Now, let children take turns being the opposite leader.

Extension: Play the game again, but this time give a verbal command that is the opposite of your action. Instruct children to try to follow your words instead of your actions. For example, say, "Stand up" while stooping low, "Swing your arms" while holding your arms tightly against yourself, "Run in place" while standing still, etc. If a child follows your action and not your words, have him sit down in his place. See if you can determine who is the best opposite listener in the group.

Over and Under

Divide the class into teams of five or six children. Have them stand in a single-file line with about 1' (30½ cm) between the players. This activity takes teamwork and brain work. The first child in line should pass the ball to the student behind him by passing the ball over his head without looking. The next child should take the ball and pass it through her legs to the student behind her. Have students continue to pass the ball down the line over and under until the child at the end of the line has the ball. This child should then run to the front of the line, leaving a little space between himself and the teammate behind him, and begin the over and under passing again. The first team to rotate through all of their teammates so that the child who began at the front of the line is again at the front is declared the "Over and Under" champion. To help them stay on track, have children call out, "Over, under, over, under, . . . " as they pass the ball.

Extension: Try this relay using other opposite passing actions. For example, have the first child rotate to his right side and pass the ball to the child behind him. Have this child rotate all the way to the left until he is nearly turned around (without turning his feet) to pass the ball to the child behind him. When a player has passed the ball, he should quickly run to the end of the line so that the passing is continuous until the team has crossed the playing area and reached a designated finish line.

Fast and Slow

Legend tells of a tortoise and a hare who once decided to race. Although it moved at a much slower pace, the tortoise won the race due to persistence and perseverance. Outline a racetrack around the edge of an outdoor play area. Have children begin running slowly like the tortoise. Tell children that every time they hear you call, "Tortoise!," they should walk as slowly as possible. When you call, "Hare!," they should run as fast as possible. Alternate the commands as children run around the racecourse.

Opposites Obstacle Course . . . .

Set up an obstacle course that explores many opposite words and actions. Some suggested obstacles might be: leap over a box, crawl under a table, hop in and out of a closet, slowly walk while balancing a book on the head, quickly run and step on each square in a hopscotch grid, etc.

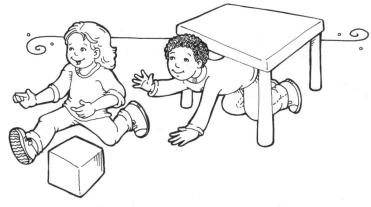

Have students complete the obstacle course forward, backward, quickly, slowly, like a mouse, like an elephant, or any other opposite ways you can imagine.

Clapping Game . . . .

This game tests listening and direction-following skills. Tell students to clap by following your instructions. Say to students, "Clap as loudly as you can, . . . now, clap as softly as you can." Other opposites to try are: fast/slow, right/left, high/low, front/back, big/little, etc.

After practicing all of the opposite options, play again. This time, do not use voice clues; instead, use only your clapping example to demonstrate each set of opposites. After the demonstration, have children guess which opposites you were clapping and then have everyone in the class join in. If you wish, allow the child who guessed correctly to perform the next opposite demonstration.

Variation: A popular invention lets you turn on televisions, lamps, or other electrical equipment simply by clapping once to turn them on and twice to turn them off. Play a clapping on and off game with the class. Each time you clap once, they should wiggle as fast and as much as possible until you clap your hands twice to "turn them off." Repeat and vary the interval between claps. Also, have students try doing specific movements (acting like a robot, pretending to be a bunny, spinning like a top, etc.) instead of just random wiggling.

Up, Down, In, Out, Around, and Through . . . .

Each child will need a plastic hoop for this activity.

As you give the commands, each child should position her body in relation to her hoop. For example, when the "up" command is given, children should raise their hoops over their heads. "Down," of course, has the opposite action. "In" indicates that children are inside the hoops, either by holding them around their waists or by placing them on the ground and stepping inside them. "Around" tells each child to balance the hoop on end on the ground, and, while holding it with one hand, circle around the hoop. "Through," of course, indicates that children should pass their bodies through the hoops.

Alternate the commands given, going faster and faster until someone gets tangled in a hoop. Add other actions like, "Swing your hoop over your head. Now, swing your hoop below your knees," "Rotate the hoop around one arm. Now, try it on the opposite side of your body," etc.

Seasons

Fall

Fall Leaves (relaxation story) . . . .

Play some soothing background music while children turn into fall leaves and move as the story directs. Use a soft, hushed voice as you read the story aloud and finish with children lying on the floor, calm and relaxed. Encourage children to move with the story as they listen to the music.

Pretend you are a leaf, high up in the air at the tippy top of a tree. You hold on tight to your branch as you enjoy the warmth of the summer sun. A gentle breeze slowly flutters over you, first one way and then another. As you glance around at the other leaves, it seems that the whole treetop is a mass of shuddering leaves.

Suddenly, you feel a prickling, tickling sensation on your back. You arch and stretch your back, trying to make the funny feeling go away. As you look over your shoulder, you notice a fuzzy caterpillar has climbed onto your back. He is crawling around with his fuzzy little feet, exploring your back. It tickles a little, and you giggle, hoping he will be done soon and move on before you start to laugh too hard.

You notice that the sun is not quite as hot today as it was yesterday, and the breeze feels a little chilly. You curl up a little as the wind blows you, slowly at first, and then faster, and faster, and faster until you have to hold on to your branch tighter than you ever have before.

As you look down, you notice that you are not quite as green as you were before; in fact, a little yellow and orange are starting to show through. You crouch down and peek around nervously from side to side, below, above, and behind you to see if the other leaves have noticed.

Day after day, you hang on to the tree limb as you get colder and turn more yellow and more orange. Today, the wind is really blowing, first one way, then the other, and now back again. It is so hard to hold on that finally you let go and quietly slip away into the sky. You are amazed at how peaceful you feel—not at all like you thought falling would be. You lean back and let the wind take you up and then down again. First you race across the sky very fast. Then, you go gently back and forth. You never know which way the wind will take you next. Finally, swirling around and around, one last gust pushes you far away and close to the ground until you float gently down and rest.

It is very peaceful on the ground. You are happy and colorful and tired. You close your eyes and dream. You dream of busy days being swept into great piles for jumping. But, for now, you are happy to bask in the sun all snuggled up with your other leaf friends.

Blowing Leaves . . . .

In the "Fall Leaves" activity, students experienced what it is like to be a falling leaf; now, they will see what it is like to be the wind. Give each child a drinking straw and a fall leaf. If you do not have real leaves, purchase artificial leaves from a craft store or cut out several using lightweight, colorful paper. Have children begin on one side of the room and move their leaves across the room by blowing on them with the straws, crawling along behind the leaves to keep them moving. Have students go from one end of the room to the other, or make it an obstacle course by maneuvering around chairs, under tables, around the trash can, etc. (If students seem to get winded or light-headed, and especially if they have asthma, try letting them create wind behind the leaves by fanning them with small paper plates.)

Leaf Trail

Cut out an assortment of large construction paper leaves in various fall colors. Tape them end-to-end on the floor in a long, winding trail. Include loops, curves, sharp corners, and long straight stretches, too. Wind the trail from one side of the room to the other, taking up as much floor space as possible. Have students start at one end and walk toe-to-toe on the leaf trail following it from beginning to end. Then, have them start at the end and walk backward to the beginning of the trail.

Variation: Have students move like floating leaves along the trail or use a pattern, such as, "hop on one foot, hop on the other foot, jump with both feet together, repeat."

Extension: Tell a story about hiking in the woods on a fall day as students walk along the trail. Have students call out what they "see" and what they are doing. Encourage them to really use their imaginations!

Raking Leaves

Instruct students to pull and drag their arms as though they are raking leaves while they say the chant.

> ### Raking Leaves
> Raking leaves is so much fun!
> First, I rake left,
> And then I rake right.
> Then, I rake in a circle
> Until I'm done!
> Rake, rake, rake,
> Rake, rake, rake,
> Rake those leaves!
> WHEEE!
> *(pretend to bend over and toss leaves in the air)*

Fall Wristbands

Using the Wristband pattern (page 50), create wristbands for all of the children with card stock or construction paper. Punch holes where indicated on each band. Use the leaf patterns to cut four to six leaves out of colorful construction paper for each child (or, use artificial leaves purchased from a craft store). Tie each leaf to a piece of string and attach through a hole in the wristband. Add long pieces of orange, yellow, red, and brown crepe paper streamers. Tell students that they can make their fall wristbands dance by gliding their arms like airplanes to float the leaves and streamers over their heads and behind them. Tell them to watch the leaves and streamers dance as they move. Remind them that it is important to move gracefully like floating leaves to avoid getting tangled. If you think it will prevent tangling, make only one wristband per child instead of two.

Wristband Pattern

Activity found on page 49.

Assembly: Have each student color and decorate a wristband and leaves. Cut out the pieces and punch holes where indicated with a black circle. Tie each leaf to a piece of string and attach the string to a hole on the wristband. Staple the wristband in a loop on the Xs.

Winter

Frozen Solid.

Talk about how slowly most things freeze. Explain that it is a gradual process that moves from the outside to the inside. Tell the class to pretend that it is winter outside, and they are going to "freeze" from top to bottom. Have them begin by wiggling and shaking as many body parts as possible. Now, tell children to freeze just their heads. (Heads stop wiggling, but the rest of the bodies stay in motion.) Continue moving down to facial features, shoulders, arms, hands, fingers, etc., until children are completely frozen down to their toes. Now, help them "thaw out" by giving the directions to unfreeze and begin wiggling again, starting with the head and working to the toes.

Jack Frost Tag

"Jack Frost" is a legendary personification of winter. He is said to bring on winter with his nimble, frozen dance across the land. Choose one child to be "Jack Frost." It is Jack Frost's job to "freeze" the other children in class by tagging them. When Jack Frost tags a child, the child must freeze in place and wait for a friend to come give him a warm, defrosting hug. If a child has been frozen three times, he cannot be unfrozen. When Jack has frozen everyone, a new Jack Frost is chosen, and the game resumes. To speed things along, you may want to choose two or three children to be Jack Frosts.

Snowball Toss.

Gather a variety of white, mismatched socks. Tie the socks into knots or roll them into balls if they are too small to tie. Have children line up next to the pile of "snowballs." Place a large box a short distance away from the group. One at a time, see how many snowballs each child can toss into the box without missing. Each time a child gets a snowball into the box, have her take a step backward before tossing the next snowball. See how far away she can get and still accurately toss a snowball. Or, let students try lobbing the socks backward over their heads into the box. Now, tell them to try tossing the snowballs into the box through their legs or with their eyes closed.

51

The Old North Wind (finger play) . . . .

Sing or chant "The Old North Wind" as you perform the finger play with students.

The Old North Wind
The Old North Wind blows this way and that;
(wave hands back and forth over head)
The Old North Wind blows off my hat.
(place hand flat on head and then lift it off)
The Old North Wind, it whistles and swirls;
(turn in a circle with arms out)
The Old North Wind freezes boys and girls!
(hug self tightly and shiver)

Mitten Dance . . . .

Gather a selection of mittens so that there is a pair for each child. Tell children that these are dancing mittens. Have them sit down, put their mittens on, and hold them very still in their laps. Explain that when you wave your arms and say the words, "Winter mittens!" their mittens should begin to dance. Play some upbeat winter music. Say, "Winter mittens!" and wave your arms over the group. Tell them that first, their mittens are timid, and they make small dancing moves in their laps and on the floor in front of them. Then, as they get warmed up, their mittens become bolder and begin waving in the air and moving along the floor to the music. Soon, their mittens become quite brave and lift them onto their feet. The mittens begin leading them around the dance floor, up and down and around and around until you say, "Winter mittens!" again, and they suddenly become ordinary mittens and drop to the floor.

Variation: Give each child one mitten. Place the matching mitten for each pair in a large basket on one side of the room. One at a time, acknowledge each child and give him an action to perform on his way across the room to find his matching mitten. Give each child a different action, such as, "Take giant steps" or "March like a soldier" to the other side of the room to retrieve his mitten.

Extension: Gather enough pairs of mittens so that there is one pair for every two children. Have children stand in a circle, facing the middle. Mix up the mittens and randomly give each child one mitten. Have each child turn her back to the circle and put on her mitten. When she turns around to face the circle again, she should hide her mittened hand behind her back. At your signal, have children begin walking around trying to find their matching mittens. When they have found their partners, they can give each other warm hugs, handshakes, or high fives.

Spring

Puddle Jump

Cut several large puddle shapes out of blue craft paper and laminate them for durability. Tape the "puddles" to the floor all over the room. Play some spring rain music, such as "Singin' in the Rain" by Gene Kelly (*Singin' in the Rain Film Soundtrack*, Rhino Records, 2002). First, have children jump over the puddles trying to avoid getting their feet "wet." Next, have them jump right in the middles of the puddles. Now, have them try jumping all around the puddles without stepping or jumping in them. Let students puddle jump another time, this time straddling each puddle with one foot on either side. How many other ways can you find to have fun with puddles?

Pick a Flower

On small strips of paper, write several different movement activities, such as "Pretend you are a cat," "Walk backward 5 steps," "Hop on one foot while saying the alphabet," "Sit, stand, sit, stand, sit, stand," "Spin around three times," etc. Tape each strip to the stem of an artificial flower (available at most craft stores). Or, you can make flowers using colorful tissue paper and pencils for the stems. Make sure that there is a flower for each child in the class. Place a square of plastic foam in the bottom of a flowerpot or bucket. Stick the flowers into the foam to create a beautiful bouquet. Let children take turns choosing flowers and leading the class in performing the activities.

Maypole Merriment

Welcome spring with May Day dancing! Construct a class maypole by attaching a long wrapping paper tube to a heavy base on the ground. Decorate the pole and top it with flowers. Then, attach several colorful crepe paper streamers, pieces of yarn, or long ribbons to the top of the pole. Have each child hold the end of a streamer and stand in a circle around the pole. Play some cheerful spring music and have students dance around the pole, allowing their streamers to twist around it. If you wish, show them how to weave in and out of each other to "braid" the streamers around the pole. As their streamers grow shorter and their circle gets tighter, tell them to switch directions and try to unwrap the streamers.

Variation: If you prefer to make this an outdoor activity, tie the streamers around a tree trunk and dance around the tree.

/\

Growing Seeds (relaxation story) . . . .

Use a soft, soothing voice while reading this story aloud. Turn out the lights and play some relaxation music in the background. You may wish to provide mats for children to lie on during this activity. Encourage them to listen to the story and move with it. You may also wish to give encouragement or suggestions to direct their movements.

Pretend that you are a seed. You are small and round and very hard. You are with all of your little seed friends in a small envelope at a store. It is dark and dry. As you look around at each one of your friends, you notice how they are all mostly just like you—but not exactly. Even though you are all small and round, you are all a little different in very special ways.

Whooosh! You feel your envelope go up quickly. Held tightly in your packet, you go up quickly, too. Someone is purchasing your little seed packet. She shakes you up and down, up and down. She shakes you hard, and then soft, fast, and then slow. She tips you one way, and all of the little seeds roll to one corner. Then, she tips the packet the other way, and you roll to the other corner. You and your seed friends make a nice rattling noise together as you rattle and tumble and bounce around inside the little seed envelope.

Suddenly, you hear a loud Rrrrriiiiiip! noise, and light begins to flood into your cozy little nook. You look up and shield your eyes from the brightness streaming in on you, and you crouch down low to avoid the light. Then, two fingers reach in and pluck you out of the envelope. "Good-bye," you softly whisper to your little seed friends as you are lifted out of the envelope and carefully dropped into a nice bed of dirt.

Wow! This bed is much softer than the envelope, and there is space to nuzzle down in the dirt without bumping another seed. This dirt feels great, and you are happy and warm as a blanket of dirt is carefully spread over the top of you. Your gardener pats the dirt once, twice, three, and four times to make sure you are safe and secure in your cozy nest. It is quiet and warm and peaceful in here. You sit for a moment and rest and listen to the muffled sounds around you. You drift off to sleep.

When you wake up, you are confused as you look around your new home. You rub your eyes and stretch and twist your head. Oh, yes, you remember, you are in a pot of dirt. But, you are not very comfortable. Your shell seems a little tight, and you begin to move about trying to stretch it out so that it will fit better. You stretch more and more until Pop! You look down and discover a root has burst out of the bottom of your shell. You wiggle it back and forth and up and down. Although you are a little worried (this root looks nothing like you after all), you still feel good. You stretch and stretch some more until Pop!—another root pops out. You stretch and wiggle this root around and move both of them together in your dirt home.

Now, you are full of energy and feel like running, but you are stuck in the dirt. It is holding you tightly, but you still feel warm, excited, and happy. Suddenly, you are growing bigger and bigger, and taller and taller, until your stem squeezes out of the dirt into the sunshine. Taller, taller, and taller still, you grow in the sun and the warm air until you can grow no more. You are stretched as far as you can stretch. Your petals reach out in every direction, and you are beautiful! You look around and see other seeds growing and stretching, and you wave an excited "Hello" to all of your friends.

Every day you stand proudly in the sun. But, one day you wake up feeling odd. You have felt this way before. Something big is going to happen. Before long, a small hand reaches around your middle and gently pulls you out of the dirt. You are jostled and rattled as a little girl quickly carries you to her mother. As you are handed to her, you feel happier than ever before. You are proud, tall, and beautiful. You are a beautiful flower, tucked in the brim of a hat, and you are ready for your next adventure!

/\

Summer

Swimming Lessons . . . .

One of the most important summer activities is the
beginning of swimming lessons. When swimming
skills are mastered, children will be able to swim
the summer away. Explain to children that you will
help them get ready for summer by having imaginary
"swimming" lessons right in the classroom. Remind
them that this activity is just for fun—they will need
to take real swimming lessons before jumping into a
real pool!

Have each child sit in a chair. The first thing to learn
is how to blow bubbles. Show children how to lean
forward and pretend to put their faces in the water.
Now, have them blow the air out of their lungs
through their mouths. When they need more air,
show them how to lift up their heads for air before
going under again for more bubbling.

Next, they will need to know how to move their
arms. Explain that when swimming forward, they
should rotate their arms forward at the shoulders
as though they are reaching for cookies. When they
grab their pretend cookies, show them how to bend
their elbows and bring the cookies back to tuck
them in their pockets. Now, have students try it with the other arm, and then again with the first, alternating
the strokes. Let them move a little faster and faster and faster. Have students try swimming the breaststroke by
drawing big imaginary hearts. Have students begin at the chest with palms pressed together, reach both arms
out in front of the body, and bring them out and around until they are back in front of the chest again.

When teaching the backstroke, there are a couple of different strokes to try. First, show children how to reach
their hands way over their heads with their elbows close to their ears. Have students alternate rotating the arms
in backward circles. For another stroke, have them pull both arms up so that their hands are in their armpits
(as if they are pretending to have chicken wings). Then, have them straighten their arms out to their sides (as
if they are acting like airplanes), and finally, they should move their arms back down to their sides. Up, out,
down, repeat.

It is now time to move those legs. Tell everyone to sit or lie on the floor for this part of the activity. Children
have probably already discovered how to do simple up and down "flutter kicks" during bath time, but everyone
should practice it together for fun. You should also show them how to do a "frog kick" by pulling their feet
up close to their bottoms while bending their knees. (This position is often called the "butterfly" in stretching
exercises.) Then, have students stick their feet out as far as possible before moving them back down again.

Everyone knows the moves, so let students lie down on the floor and practice swimming to some favorite beach
songs, such as "Baby Beluga" by Raffi (*Baby Beluga*, Rounder/Pgd, 1996)—kicking and stroking at the same
time, fast, slow, on the tummy, and on the back. Remind them to blow bubbles and breathe, too. Now, you can
even have an imaginary swim meet!

Extension: Have more "swimming" fun with flipper relay races. A student can put on swim flippers and
speed walk or run to a designated point where a teammate is waiting. He should hand off his flippers to that
teammate, who should return to the other line and hand off the flippers again. Continue until all of the team
members have completed the relay.

Fishing for Fun . . . .

Using the Fish pattern (page 57), cut out 10 construction-paper fish. Place a metal paper clip on the mouth of each fish. Write a number, 1 through 10, on one side of each fish and an action word or phrase on the other side of the fish. Spread out the fish on the floor in an imaginary "pond." You may want to separate the pond from children with a curtain. Make a fishing pole with a magnet tied to the end of the string. Let children take turns fishing for two fish. Read the number off of the first fish and the activity off of the second fish to determine what students will be doing. For example, if a child pulls out one fish with a number 6 on it and a second fish with the words "jumping jacks" on it, the whole class would do six jumping jacks. Toss the fish back into the pond and invite a second child to go fishing!

Beach Ball Boogie . . . .

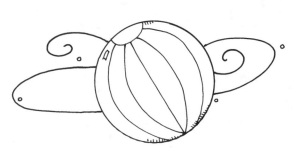

Inflate a small beach ball for each child or each pair of children. Play selections from a beach party album, such as *Catch a Wave: Beach Songs for Kids* (Music Little People, 2000), and have boogie game time! Have children try nudging the beach balls across the room with their foreheads or noses while crawling on their hands and knees. Or, a student can bounce it back and forth with a friend. Tell them to try to balance the ball on one hand while standing on one foot. They can also lie on the floor with their legs in the air and try to balance the balls on top of their feet. Have all sorts of balancing boogie fun with beach balls.

Surf's Up. . . . .

Cut out a surfboard shape from a large poster board for each child in the class. Have them color and personalize their own surfboards as desired. Play some great surfing music, such as "Surfin' Safari" by The Beach Boys (*Surfin' Safari*, Capitol Records, 2001), and show them how to "hang ten" on their boards (stand on the front end of the board with all 10 toes hanging over the edge). Then, have them lie on their stomachs and "paddle out." When they get to good "waves," tell them to stand up and balance on their boards, one foot in front of the other until they ride the waves successfully or wipe out. Let students continue swimming, surfing, and dancing with the boards until the end of the song.

Fish Pattern

Activity found on page 56.

CD-104041 *It's Wiggle Time!*

ΛΛΛΛΛΛΛΛΛΛΛΛΛΛΛΛΛΛΛΛΛΛΛΛΛΛΛΛΛΛΛΛΛΛΛΛΛΛΛΛΛΛΛΛΛΛΛ

Ring Toss . . . .

Gather several inflatable float rings—preferably one per child. Play selections from a beach party album, such as *Catch a Wave: Beach Songs for Kids* (Music Little People, 2000), and let children have fun dancing with the rings around their waists. Now, let them try some other fun activities with the rings. Have each student:

- ❀ hold it high over her head.
- ❀ put it on one foot and dance and twirl it around.
- ❀ spin it on one hand and then pass it to the other, continuing to twirl it.
- ❀ slip an arm through the middle of the ring and through another child's ring at the same time.
- ❀ dance with a friend as doubled-up dancers.
- ❀ throw the ring up into the air and catch it on one arm.
- ❀ toss the ring like a flying disk and then have a friend toss it back.
- ❀ roll the ring along the ground until it tips over.
- ❀ bump into others while wearing a ring around her waist and see what happens.

Extension: Designate several targets around the playground by marking them with big, masking-tape letter Xs. The targets might include a tree, the side of the building, the top of the slide, etc. Have children travel around the playground trying to hit each target by tossing the rings like flying disks at each target. Have the last target be a T-ball tee and see if anyone can toss a ring over the tee from a few feet away.

Summertime Hot and Cold. . . . .

Tell children that you will name an item or a situation that is either hot or cold, and they should act out that scenario. Tell them that you want them to think first and then act when you give the signal. You may wish to model a few of the activities with them until they feel comfortable with the concept. Here are a few suggestions to get you started. Ask them, "What would you look like if you were . . . ":

- ❀ . . . walking on hot pavement with bare feet?
- ❀ . . . an ice cube in a glass of lemonade?
- ❀ . . . an ice cream cone that has been left in the sun?
- ❀ . . . walking in the hot sand to get across the beach?

ΛΛΛΛΛΛΛΛΛΛΛΛΛΛΛΛΛΛΛΛΛΛΛΛΛΛΛΛΛΛΛΛΛΛΛΛΛΛΛΛΛΛΛΛΛΛΛ

Shapes

Shape Bodies . . . .

Who can make a circle with their bodies? First, have students try to make little ones with their hands, then bigger ones with their arms, and then even bigger ones with their whole bodies. Explore the many different ways to bend and stretch the body to make various shapes while standing, sitting, or lying on the floor. Repeat the activity with several different shapes. Give suggestions where needed and have children try to imitate a particularly unique or successful way of creating a shape. Depending on children's developmental levels, you may want to make copies of the Shape Cards (page 61) to use as visual aids during this activity.

Extension: Have the class work in teams to create shapes. Have the rest of the class see if they can guess which shape each team has made.

Shape Hop . . . .

Use masking tape to create circles, squares, triangles, and rectangles on the floor. (Include more shapes if desired.) Make some shapes very large and some much smaller.

Have students dance to a favorite music selection. Periodically, stop the music and announce the name of a shape. Each child should stop dancing and rush to put one foot on the shape you called. Vary the shapes and directions given. For example, have them put their hands into the small circles or sit in the biggest square, etc.

Extension: To challenge students, use colorful masking or electrical tape when making the shapes so that they are now looking for the shape and the color that you call out.

Shape of Me . . . .

Have children sing or chant the following rhyme while performing the movements.

Shape of Me

I can make a triangle,   *(bend arm at elbow and place it on the hip)*
I can touch the floor,   *(touch the floor)*
I can make a circle,   *(reach hands over head, round the arms, and touch the fingertips)*
And do a whole lot more.

I can make a square,   *(squat in ball and place arms across legs, one at knees, one at feet)*
Rectangles are longer still.   *(stand straight like a soldier)*
If you ask if I can make a shape of me,
I can answer, "I will!"   *(stomp foot and jump up with arms in the air)*

Shape Corners . . . .

Tape a large circle in one corner of the room, a square in another corner, a triangle in a third corner, and a rectangle in a fourth corner.

Make enough Shape Cards (page 61) of the four basic shapes (circle, triangle, square, and rectangle) so that there is at least one card per child. Lay the cards facedown in the middle of the room. Choose an action for each shape. For example, the square might be the "wild-arms-and-legs" shape. The circle could be the "ball-bouncing" shape. The triangle could be the "baby-walking" shape, and the rectangle could be the "floating-scarves" shape. Any activity will do, just be sure to choose a variety of active and relaxed motions. Demonstrate the actions in each of the shape corners before beginning.

To begin, play a favorite music selection and have everyone select a Shape Card from the middle of the room. Those who choose a square card will go to the large square. Those who choose circle cards will go to the large circle, and so on, until all of the children are in their corners. Give students one minute to perform the activities in their shape corners and then give a signal. Have children return their cards to the middle of the room and select new cards. They then go to the new corners and try the new movements. Let students continue drawing cards and moving. Play the game again with a new set of actions for the shape corners. When children are moving from one corner to the next, you may want to call out a silly dance move or other fun way to transition.

Move It Shape Race . . . .

If a circle, a triangle, and a square were having a race, how would each one move? As a group, discuss the different ways each shape might move. For instance, a circle would probably roll or somersault across the play area. A square might move by walking like a duck—crouched down with the knees at sharp angles. A triangle might walk like a caterpillar by bringing its back end up close to its front end with its middle stuck way up in the air. Then, it would stretch its front end forward, flattening out before bringing up its back end again.

When students have determined and practiced the walking style of each shape, divide children into three groups and designate one group for each shape. Mark start and finish lines. At your signal, have a relay race between the three teams. Which shape is the fastest? Which is the slowest? Try the relay again, but this time, trade shapes. Choose a new movement for each shape and start over if desired.

Shape Dance. . . . .

Each child needs a set of three large shapes—a circle, a square, and a triangle—cut out of colorful construction paper. Or, you can enlarge the Shape Cards (page 61). You may wish to laminate the shapes for durability. Tape each child's group of three shapes to the floor with plenty of space between the shapes, allowing room to dance. Have children stand next to their shapes. Tell them that they should hop on the shapes as you sing the shapes' names. Each time you sing a name, children should hop; so, if you sing, "circle" twice in a row, children should hop on their circles twice.

Try these two "Shape Dance" songs and then create your own for more dancing fun!

> **Sing to the tune of "Old MacDonald"**
> Circle, circle, tri-an-gle.
> Square, square, square, square, square.
>
> **Sing to the tune of "Mary Had a Little Lamb"**
> Cir-cle, cir-cle, tri-an-gle,
> Tri-an-gle, tri-an-gle.
> Cir-cle, cir-cle, tri-an-gle,
> Square, cir-cle, tri-an-gle.

Shape Cards

Activities found on pages 59–60.

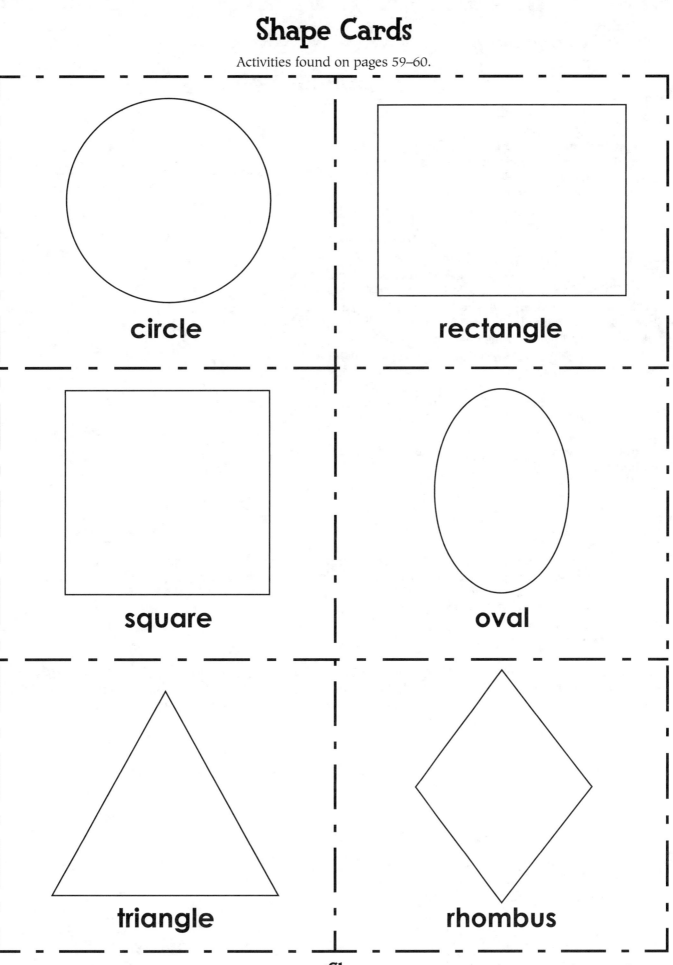

circle

rectangle

square

oval

triangle

rhombus

Space

Force Field

In the movies, many spaceships have force field protection capabilities while traveling in space. This means that an invisible shield surrounds the spaceship and protects it from any oncoming danger. In a large, open play area, tell students to pretend they are spaceships blasting off into space with the latest force field capabilities. As they fly through the air as fast as they can, the "force fields" require that they steer clear of any objects in their airspace—including other spaceships, planets, or space junk. Explain that aliens, on the other hand, will try to destroy the force fields by trying to bump into the "spaceships." Choose two children to be aliens. Use the pattern (page 63) to make Alien Headbands for them to wear. Have an open space flying practice, with "aliens" darting about trying to neutralize each spaceship's force field by tagging it. When a spaceship's force field is compromised, it must return to the space station (a designated waiting area). Continue playing until there is one spaceship remaining. Designate new aliens and begin again.

Variation: Create a space obstacle course of objects to fly around, over, and under. Have students focus on going as fast as possible while being very careful not to touch anyone or anything.

Walking on the Moon

Cut 20 large moon-boot-shaped footprints out of construction paper. Laminate them for durability. Talk with students about the lack of gravity on the moon. This means that walking takes great effort because a person's legs feel like they are going to fly off into space with every step. Astronauts wear big, heavy boots to help them stay on the ground while they walk on the moon. Also, discuss the fact that there is little atmosphere on the moon, so there is no wind or water to sweep away footprints. When a footprint has been made on the moon, it will stay there for a very long time.

Choose one child to create a path to follow using the footprints. Encourage him to take large moon steps as he places the footprints where he steps. Have the rest of the class follow the first astronaut's footprints by walking like astronauts through the footprint trail. Remind students that astronauts move very slowly and deliberately. Have the last astronaut collect the footprints and start the next moon walk trail.

Extension: Cut three sets of footprints that are obviously different sizes. Make three trails that cross over and circle around each other. Encourage children to follow each of the three footprint paths. Depending on students' developmental levels, you may want to make the three sets of footprints using three different colors.

Alien Headband Pattern

Activity found on page 62.

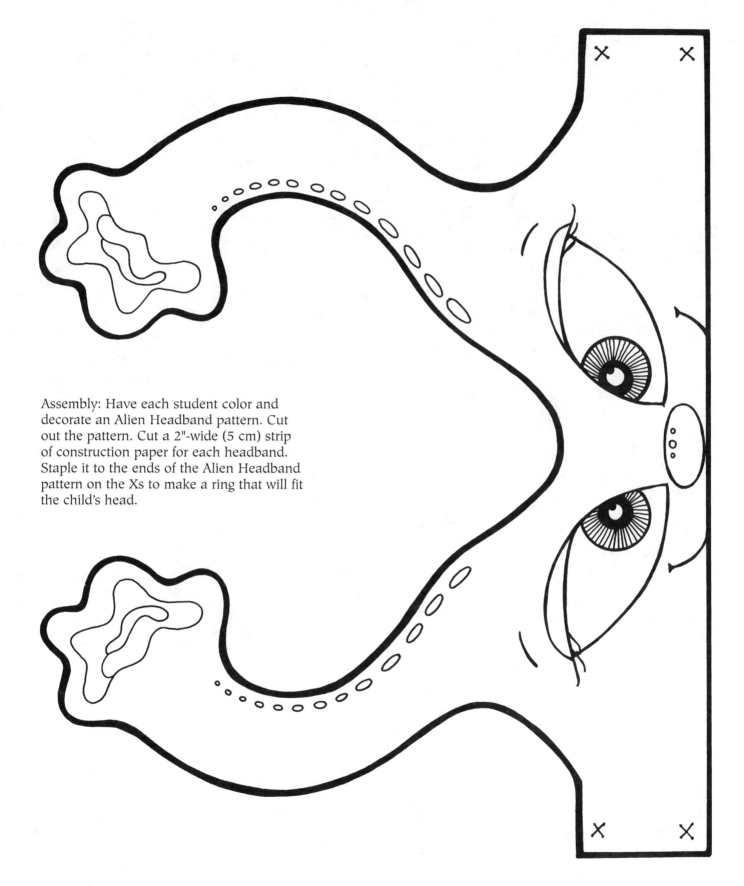

Assembly: Have each student color and decorate an Alien Headband pattern. Cut out the pattern. Cut a 2"-wide (5 cm) strip of construction paper for each headband. Staple it to the ends of the Alien Headband pattern on the Xs to make a ring that will fit the child's head.

CD-104041 *It's Wiggle Time!*

Shooting Stars

As stars burn up, they shoot quickly through the atmosphere. Trace a star on the bottom of a heavy paper plate for each student. Have children decorate the stars with markers or crayons. If desired, add some crepe paper streamers around the edges of the plates. Let students take the stars outside and make them fly across the play area by throwing them like flying disks. See if they can make their shooting stars land on or hit specific targets. See how far they can make their stars travel. Let them experiment with different ways of throwing the stars.

Star Hopping

Tape several large, star-shaped outlines on the floor. You will need one star for every five students. Have each student stand on a point of a star. Instruct children that every time you signal, they should run, walk, hop, skip, crawl, etc., as directed around the outlines to the next points and stop. This activity can also be done with music playing in the background.

Variation: Have students take turns walking along the outlines of the stars while racing the clock. Give each student 20 seconds to complete the star the first time and take a few seconds off for each successive try. Ring a bell when the star-tracing time is up.

Starlight Wishes

Make a starlight wand by covering a cardboard star with foil. Attach the star to a dowel or a cardboard tube and add metallic streamers and chenille craft sticks for decoration. Invite one child to be the starlight wisher. Explain that many people believe that making a wish when the first star of the evening appears will make the wish come true. Let students repeat the following poem:

> ***Star Light, Star Bright***
> Star light, star bright,
> first star I see tonight.
> I wish I may, I wish I might,
> have the wish I wish tonight.

Have the starlight wisher whisper an action into your ear that she wishes the rest of the class to perform. Say to the class, "_____ wishes for you to do 10 jumping jacks." Have the starlight wisher lead the class in her wish and then wave the wand over the next student to make a wish. Or, you can reverse the activity. Whisper an activity into a child's ear so that she can tell the class what your wish is, and then let her lead the class in performing it.

Sports

Tennis

To make a simple "tennis racket," stretch and bend a wire hanger into a diamond shape. Bend the hook into a loop for a handle. Stretch the toe of a clean nylon stocking over the diamond-end of the hanger and pull it tight. Knot the stocking where the diamond meets the handle. Use duct tape to secure the stocking in place and cover any sharp edges on the hanger. Obtain several small foam balls to use as tennis balls.

Divide children into pairs and have them volley back and forth to each other. Make a "net" by stretching a piece of yarn across the backs of two chairs. Or, give each child her own "ball" and have her see if she can bounce it high, low, fast, slow, etc. See who can keep a ball bouncing continuously for the longest time.

Golfer's Delight

Drill a hole in the side of an empty tin can or plastic soda bottle. Insert a long dowel or a cardboard wrapping paper tube and secure with duct tape to create a putter. Use plastic golf balls. If you think it will be easier for children, substitute larger balls, such as plastic, hole-filled practice baseballs. Remind children that golfers never swing their putters above their knees.

Build a nine-hole golf course by creating several hazards and obstacles. Some suggestions:

- ❀ Remove both ends of an empty coffee or paint can and have students putt through the open cylinder.
- ❀ Duct tape several "can cylinders" together and let students putt through the tube.
- ❀ Create an incline/decline by propping pieces of cardboard on small boxes or blocks.
- ❀ Let students putt under a desk, around a chair, etc.
- ❀ Place two rows of blocks down the middle of the "green" and have students practice putting in between them.
- ❀ Make the paths more complicated by setting up boundaries with masking tape lines.
- ❀ Build sand traps and water hazards by placing blankets or towels in bunches on the floor.
- ❀ Create the "cup" at the end of each hole by securing an empty coffee or paint can to the ground with duct tape.

T-ball

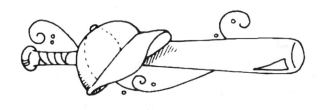

Set up a small baseball field with three bases, a home plate, and a small tee. Use a plastic, hole-filled ball and a small plastic bat. Have one child come up to bat while the rest of the group spreads out in the field. As the batter hits and then runs the bases, have the other players try to field the ball. Explain that there are no outs—everyone gets to run the bases. Whoever fields the ball becomes the next batter, and the previous batter takes his place in the field. You may need to rotate field positions so that everyone gets a chance to field the ball and bat.

Soccer

Obtain several soccer balls, sized for the preschool-kindergarten age group. Have children practice dribbling (moving the ball with several short, light kicks). Next, have them stand still while you gently roll the ball to them. See if they can kick the rolling ball back to you. Finally, set the ball a short distance from a goal and see if they can kick the ball into the goal.

No-Tackle Football

Running: Mark a goal line and a start line. Have children line up on the start line. Give each child a different play, such as, "Go long" (run close to the goal, then turn to catch the ball), "Short pass" (run a short distance, then turn to catch the ball), "Slant left" (run diagonally to the left and toward the goal, then turn to catch the ball), etc. Let each child score a touchdown as you play quarterback.

Passing: Divide the class into teams of three. Have one child from each team be the center (the person who hikes the ball to the quarterback), one be the quarterback (the person who takes the ball from the center and throws it), and one be the receiver (the person who catches the ball). Have each quarterback line up behind a center. Tell the quarterbacks to say, "One, two, three, hike!" at which point each center should pass the ball through her legs to the quarterback. The quarterback should step back and throw the ball to the receiver down the field.

Kicking: Place the ball on the ground several yards from the established goal line. See how many kicks it takes for each student to get the ball from one end of the field to the goal line.

Keep track of the group score (one point for each time someone crosses the goal line) and give many high fives.

Track and Field

Relay: Divide the class in half. Have the two groups line up on opposite sides of the play area. Decorate a cardboard tube as desired and use it as a baton. At your signal, the first child in line on one side should take the baton and run to the other end of the play area to pass it to the first child in that line. Have players continue running back and forth passing the baton until the entire class has had a chance to run. Time them as they run the relay. Rest for a minute and then let students run again to try to beat their first time.

Shot Put: Obtain several beanbags or small rubber playground balls. Depending on students' developmental levels, you may want to use foam balls for this activity. Draw a large circle on the ground. One at a time, have students stand in the circle and throw a "shot put" as far as they can. Mark each student's distance and see if she can beat her first try. If you wish, show them proper shot put form—throwing from the shoulder, using spinning momentum to throw farther, etc.

Hurdles: Place several small boxes or other objects on the ground about 4' (1 1/4 m) apart in a long row. You may prefer to use masking tape lines if you are worried about tripping. Encourage each child to run and jump over the hurdles by leaping over them with one foot outstretched.

Long Jump: Mark a starting line and a take-off line about 10' (3 m) apart. Have children line up at the starting line. At your signal, have the first child run to the take-off line and jump as far as possible. Use a piece of masking tape to mark the landing spot. Measure the distance of the jump from the take-off line to the landing point. Record the results and send the next jumper. Add all of the measurements together to see how far the whole class jumped.

Transportation

Vamoose Caboose! . . . .

Divide children into teams of three and have each team line up single file. Have each child hold on to the waist of the child in front of him to create a train. At your signal, have each "train" head out of the "station" across the "track." As the engine picks up steam, have the first child pump her arms faster and faster. Explain that as the engine winds and turns its way along, chances are, she might lose the caboose. If the caboose (the child at the back of the train) lets go or gets lost, he must quickly find another train of children to join. After a few minutes, stop and have the team members switch so that everyone gets a chance to be an engine and a caboose.

Variation: As the trains chug around the play area, have them listen for the train whistle. When they hear you give the signal (blow on a train whistle or make a "toot, toot" noise), all of the cabooses should separate and scramble to find other trains to join.

Locomotion Commotion . . . .

Have one child sit against the wall with his legs in front of him in a V-shape. Have the next child sit right in front of the first child in the same position. Continue lining children in front of each other until the entire class is tucked together with legs extended. Tell each child to place her hands on the waist of the child in front of her. You can be the engine. Tell children that you are going to move this train up a hill, and you need everyone's help. Sit in the front of the line, and as the class makes train noises, have everyone simultaneously lift his right leg and "scoot" forward on his bottom as he places his leg down again on the ground. Repeat with the left leg, slowly moving faster and faster until the entire train has traveled across the room. Break children into smaller teams to have lots of Locomotion Commotion all over the room. If it helps them pick up steam, children can chant, "I think I can, I think I can," as they move forward.

Variation: Using the same seating posture, create your own roller coaster. Instead of using the legs, this activity involves upper body motions. Have everyone in line hold her hands up and lean back on the way "up" the first "hill" while making "click-clack" climbing sounds. Then, have them hold on to the people in front of them as you career "down" a hill (leaning forward as far as possible), then back up the next hill (lean back again). Next, pretend there is a sharp, banking turn to the left and then to the right. Have students continue leaning for the hills and turns and adding appropriate sound effects until you come to an abrupt "stop" at the end of the "ride." You can also do this as an airplane ride with arms extended to the sides as you climb, dive, dip, and swoop through the clouds.

Road Signs . . . .

As you drive a car, there are numerous signs and warnings to observe in order to drive safely. Enlarge and color the Road Sign Cards (page 69) so that each sign is large enough to be seen by all of the children. Go over all of the signs and their meanings (see list below) so that everyone knows what to do when a sign is displayed. Play some driving music, such as "409" by The Beach Boys (*Little Deuce Coupe*, Capitol Records, 2001), and show children how to drive their "cars" by holding imaginary steering wheels in front of them while jogging lightly with their feet. Remind them not to speed and that they must always obey traffic signs or they will get tickets or have accidents. Have children pretend to turn the keys in the ignitions of their cars. Display the green light signal to get them started. After a short period of "driving," display one of the other traffic signs and notify the class of the change. Each sign has a different action associated with it. Be sure to enforce all "traffic laws" and "revoke" any "licenses" for "reckless driving."

- ❀ **Stop Sign:** Stop driving and freeze.
- ❀ **Green Light Signal:** Begin driving.
- ❀ **Left Turn:** Turn in circles to the left.
- ❀ **Right Turn:** Turn in circles to the right.
- ❀ **Dead End:** Back up.
- ❀ **One Way:** Drive only in the direction that the arrow points.
- ❀ **Yield:** Slow down.
- ❀ **Slippery When Wet:** Slip and slide around the room.

Bike Ride (imagination exploration) . . . .

Narrate and act out the instructions in the dialogue below as you take the class for a "bike ride."

Today, we are going to take a bike ride in the countryside. First, we need to pick out our "bikes." I am going to take a red one. What color is yours, _____? *(Individually ask each child to answer.)* Now, put up the "kickstands" and swing your legs over the "seats." Put on your "helmets." Test your "horns." We're ready to go!

(Begin by holding your arms at 90° angles as if gripping the handlebars and "pedal" by rotating your legs in a circular motion as you march forward.) Sit up straight and stay close. We do not want to lose anyone! Follow me. *(Lead children around the play area, taking easy curves and winding back and forth.)* I "see" a cow enjoying the pasture over there. What do you see? *(Allow everyone to share the things that they see along the bike ride. If you wish, individually call out names and ask them what they see.)*

(Hold up your hand to tell everyone to stop.) We are at a "crosswalk." We need to get off of our bikes to safely cross the "street." *(Climb off of the bike, look both ways, and then proceed to walk your bike across the street.)* Now that everyone is safely across, we can "ride" again. *(Climb back on the bike and begin riding again.)*

Wow! This "hill" is really steep. My legs are working so hard to get me to the top. *(Pedal slowly and deliberately as if pedaling uphill, breathing hard.)* Whew! We made it! Now, we can "coast" down the hill to that grassy area down there. OK, let's "park" our bikes here and rest. We can lie in the grass and look at clouds. *(Have children tell you what the clouds look like.)* What a wonderful day for a bike ride! We have seen . . . *(Have children help you list several of the things you saw along the way on the bike ride.)* We better get home; it is getting late. Everyone go back to your bikes, and let's go home.

Variation: Play some music with various tempos (see the Music Selection Collection on page 80) and have children lie on their backs with their knees bent at 90° angles. Now, have them lift their hips up off of the ground, supporting their backs with their arms, and begin pedaling in the air. Show them how to pedal hard and fast when the music has a rapid beat and slow and smooth when the music has a slow beat.

Road Sign Cards

Activity found on page 68.

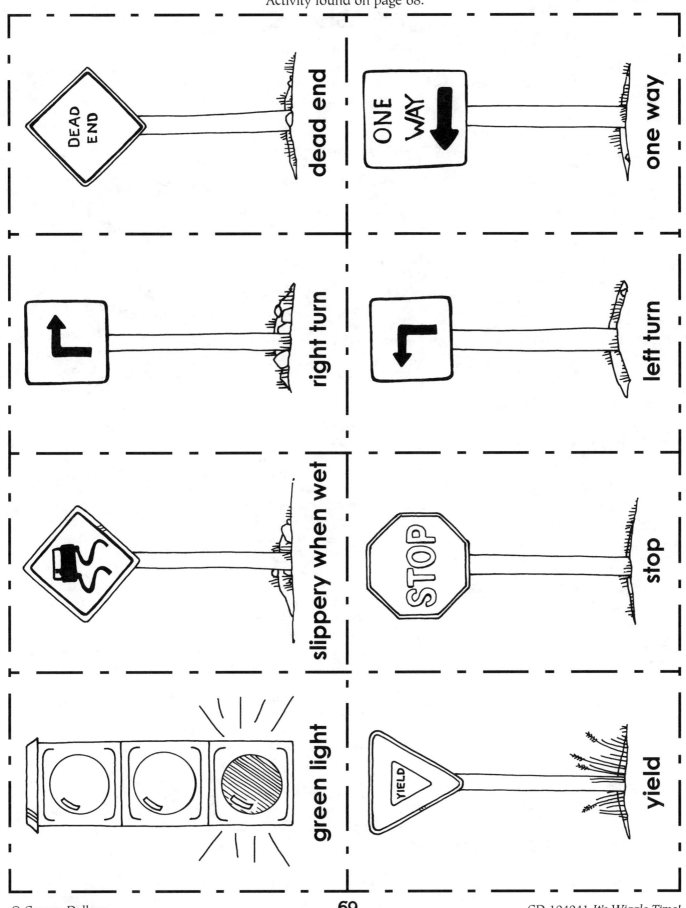

dead end

one way

right turn

left turn

slippery when wet

stop

green light

yield

CD-104041 *It's Wiggle Time!*

Weather

Storm Dance . . . .

Rain falling, wind blowing, lightning crashing—and that's just the noise a storm makes outside! Sing or chant "The Progression of a Storm" as you lead students in creating an indoor storm dance.

The Progression of a Storm

The wind picks up . . .	*(move around as if blown by the wind)*
The clouds roll in . . .	*(lie down and roll across the room)*
It begins to sprinkle . . .	*(rub fingers together, softly tap toes)*
The rain comes down . . .	
Faster and faster.	*(clap progressively louder and faster)*
A crack of lightning	
Slices through the sky!	*(clap twice and leap side to side)*
Thunder rolls . . .	*(stomp feet and pound a tabletop)*
Hail pounds . . .	*(pound or stomp on the floor)*
The rain slows, then stops.	*(clap progressively softer and slower)*
The wind stops blowing;	*(slow the breezy movements until very still)*
The clouds move on;	*(roll across the room)*
The sun shines again.	*(lie quietly on the back and sigh)*

Windy Day . . . .

Using a fan and a piece of paper or a plastic grocery bag, show children what things look like when they blow around in the wind. Create a weather vane using a wooden dowel or a pencil and the Weather Vane pattern (page 71). Show children how a weather vane works. (It always points in the direction that the wind is blowing.) So, if the weather vane is pointing to the right, then the wind is blowing to the right.

Stand in front of the class with the weather vane. Tell them that they are going to be blown by the wind, but they must watch the weather vane to know which way to go. Turn the weather vane in one direction while the whole class "blows" to one side of the room. Remind them how the paper and the plastic bag moved when they were blowing around so that children will move similarly. Now, point the weather vane in the other direction until the entire class has blown and tumbled to the opposite side of the room. Point the weather vane in an entirely new direction, sending students off on a new tangent. Change the direction of the weather vane mid-romp to a whole new direction or spin the weather vane in circles to indicate a swirling wind. Invite children to take turns being the weather vane controller.

Weather Vane Pattern

Activity found on page 70.

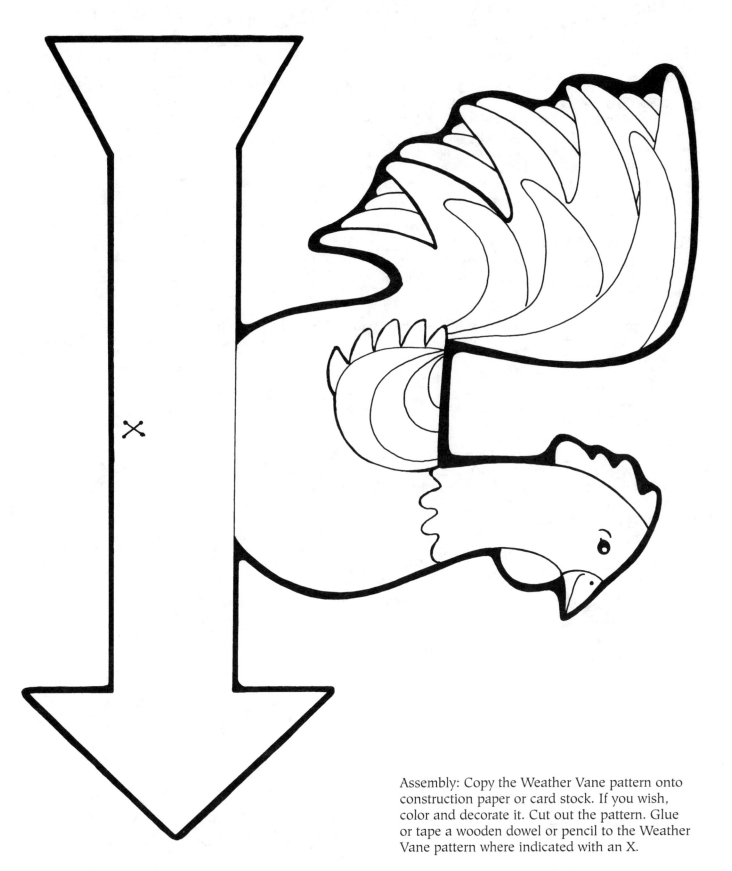

Assembly: Copy the Weather Vane pattern onto construction paper or card stock. If you wish, color and decorate it. Cut out the pattern. Glue or tape a wooden dowel or pencil to the Weather Vane pattern where indicated with an X.

 CD-104041 *It's Wiggle Time!*

ʌ∧

Drifting Clouds . . . .

Sometimes on a nice day, it is fun to lie in the grass and look at the puffy white clouds. Talk to children about how they can use their imaginations to visualize familiar objects in the clouds.

Choose three or four children to be a "cloud team." In a whisper, give the team a suggested action, such as, "Act like fish." Have the team start at one side of the room and slowly drift across the room in front of the class. When they get in front of the rest of the group, ring a bell or give a signal for them to stop. When the cloud team stops, they should all act like the object you have suggested. See if the class can figure out what the "cloud" is by their actions. Continue until all of the children have had opportunities to be parts of "clouds."

Snowy, Cloudy, Rainy, Sunny . . . .

Enlarge the Weather Cards (page 73) and cut them apart. Color and laminate them if desired. Hold up one card and teach children the action for that card. Repeat with the other three cards.

- ❋ **Snowy**: Lift up and down onto tiptoes while floating arms through the air.
- ❋ **Cloudy**: Crouch down into a tight ball.
- ❋ **Rainy**: Hold hands over head as if protecting self from rain while running quickly in place.
- ❋ **Sunny**: Hold arms out open wide, bend head back as if basking in the sun, and sigh, "Ahhh!"

Place all four Weather Cards facedown in front of you. Tell children that each time you say a weather word and show the card, they should act out that word as shown above until you say and show the next card. Very slowly, hold up one card at a time while children perform the associated activities. Gradually increase the speed of the game by saying the words in random order more and more quickly. See how quickly children can respond before they melt into puddles of giggles and confusion.

Variation: To make the game easier, choose a one-action response for each word, such as clap, stomp, nod, or twirl.

Extension: To make the game more challenging, make up new actions for each weather pattern or add more weather words to the sequence.

ʌ∧

CD-104041 *It's Wiggle Time!*

Weather Cards

Activity found on page 72.

sunny

rainy

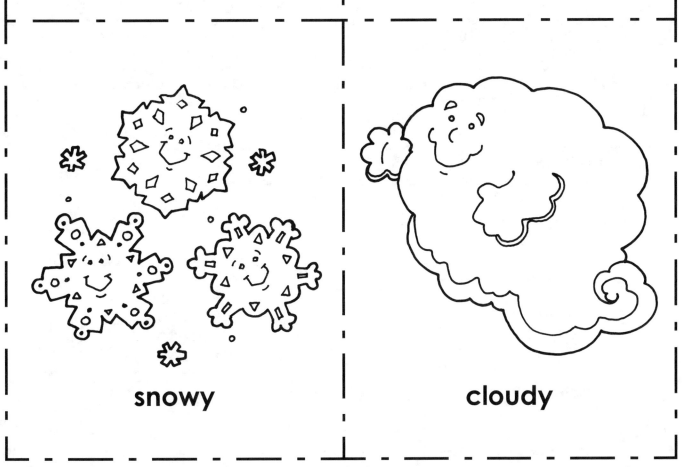

snowy

cloudy

Zoo Animals

Walk like the Animals. . . . .

Enlarge the Zoo Animal Cards (pages 75–77) and cut them apart. Color and laminate them if desired. Have one child choose a card from the pile and secretly look at it. Depending on children's developmental levels, you may need to secretly discuss the mannerisms of the selected animal with each child. Have the child walk or act like that animal. The rest of the class should try to guess which animal the child is imitating, and then have everyone in the class join in to act like the animal. Repeat until everyone has had a turn or until all of the cards are gone.

Variation: Select a card from the stack. After noting the animal on the card, say, "If I were you, and I lived in the zoo . . . " then add a phrase that highlights a distinguishing characteristic of the animal you selected. For example, if you choose a card that says "flamingo," you might say, "If I were you, and I lived in the zoo, I would stand around all day on one leg." If children cannot guess the animal from your first clue, add a second clue by repeating the first and adding the second: "If I were you, and I lived in the zoo, I would stand around all day on one leg, and I would be pink." Continue adding clues until children can guess the animal you are describing. Then, have children act like the chosen animal. Choose a new card and play again.

Extension: Divide the room into four or five different "habitat" sections. You may want to make physical dividers for your habitats by taping off boxes on the floor or making paths of wooden blocks. Divide the class so that there are a few children in each habitat area. Assign one group to be the monkeys, another to be the elephants, a third to be the bears, the fourth group to be lions and tigers, and the fifth group to be flamingos. Encourage children in each habitat to act like their group animals. Invite another class from school to visit the "zoo." See if they can guess which "animals" are in the zoo. Choose new animals and invite another group to visit.

Extension: Have each child select a card. Using construction paper, markers, yarn, etc., give each child time to create a mask or paper bag costume of her animal. Then, wearing the costumes, students can act like their animals or inhabit the class zoo as described in the above activity.

Zoo Animal Cards

Activity found on page 74.

tiger

lion

bear

elephant

seal

flamingo

giraffe

chimpanzee

Zoo Animal Cards

Activity found on page 74.

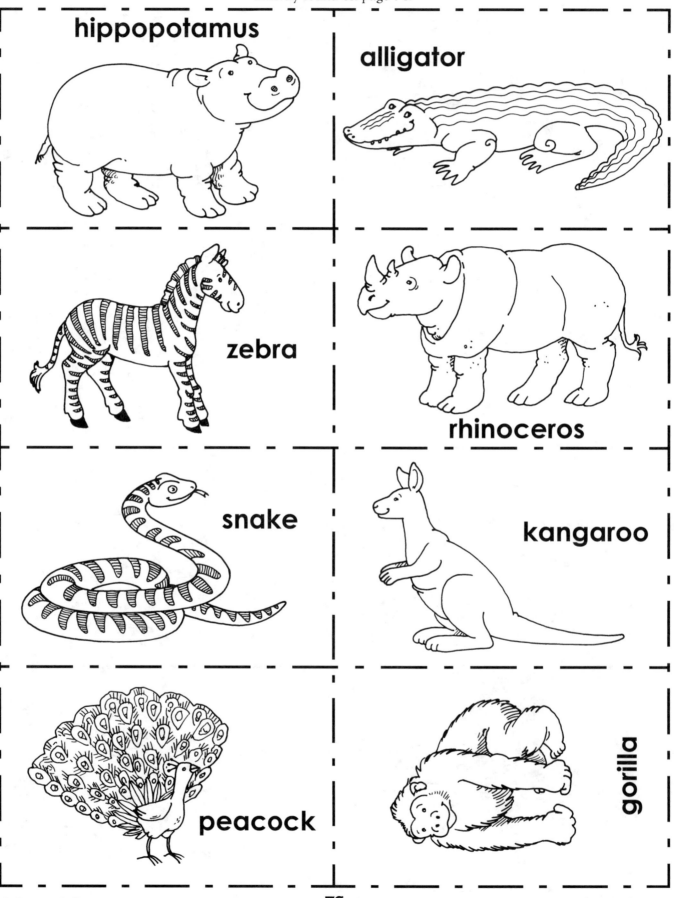

hippopotamus

alligator

zebra

rhinoceros

snake

kangaroo

peacock

gorilla

CD-104041 *It's Wiggle Time!*

Zoo Animal Cards

Activity found on page 74.

turtle

owl

turkey

warthog

rabbit

frog

duck

parrot

CD-104041 *It's Wiggle Time!*

Frogs and Alligators . . . .

Alligators are known for their quickness and their powerful jaws. To be successful in this game, the "frogs" must get all of the way around the room without getting caught by the "alligator" that is waiting just under the water.

Cut out several lily pads of varying sizes using large, green construction paper. Tape them to the floor in a big circle, about 18" (46 cm) apart so that they are close enough to step across, but far enough apart that children have to stretch a little to make it to the next lily pad.

Choose one child to be the alligator, waiting in the middle of the pond. Have the frogs take turns moving from one lily pad to the next around the circle. If a frog steps off of a lily pad into the "water," the alligator must be alert enough to see it happen and call out the frog's name. If the alligator is successful in "catching" a frog in the water, the frog becomes the next alligator. When the frogs seem to have mastered their trip around the lily pads, have them move faster and faster or try various ways of getting from one lily pad to the next, such as hopping only on one foot or leapfrogging.

Tiger Tail Tag . . . .

Each child needs a scarf or bandana to use as a tail. Have students tuck their "tails" into their back pockets or in the waistbands of their pants. If no pocket or waistband is available, tape the tail to the child's back.

At your signal, have the "tiger cubs" begin "prowling" around the room. You can choose to have the tigers play while crawling on all fours or standing up. The object of the game is similar to capture the flag—collect other tigers' tails by gently tugging them from the pockets. The trick is for one tiger to steal another tiger's tail without losing his own! If a tiger loses his own tail, he is out for that round. Play until all but one or two children have lost their tails. Redistribute the tails and play again.

Variation: Have one child stand and be the tiger tamer while the rest of the children play tigers, crawling around with their bandana tails. Play begins with your signal, but this time, only the tiger tamer is tugging tails. After a given amount of time, the tiger tamer lines up all of the tigers he has caught and teaches them a new trick of his choice, such as rolling over, sitting up, roaring on command, etc.

Lions and Tigers and Bears . . . .

Mark start and finish lines on opposite sides of the room. Have the class line up on the start line. Choose a small stuffed lion, tiger, or bear. Have one child leave the room while another hides the animal. When the player who left the room returns, have the class quietly chant while tiptoeing one step at a time toward the finish line, "Lions and tigers and bears, oh my!" (Have students throw hands in the air when saying, "Oh my!") The chant should grow gradually louder as the child who is looking gets closer and closer to the hidden animal. When the animal is finally found, the rest of the children should quickly run to the finish line and sit down. The last child to find a seat is "captured" by the animal and must sit out for one round. If children reach the finish line before the item is found, everyone returns to the beginning and the child who was looking gets captured and must sit out a turn.

78

Zoo Rap

Sing or chant the "Zoo Rap" while performing the motions.

Zoo Rap

I went to the zoo the other day,	*(hold right hand out to side)*
And this is what the animals	*(hold left hand out to side)*
Had to say . . .	*(put both hands to mouth)*
The snakes said, "Hiss!"	*(move hand up and down in a wave across body)*
The zebra said, "Eeep! Eeep!"	*(stomp one foot and toss head back)*
The birds said, "Chirp!"	*(move index finger and thumb together in front of mouth)*
And, "Eedle-deedle-deep."	*(flap arms and walk in a circle)*
Zoo rap, zoo rap, eedle-deedle doo rap!	*(dance)*
Zoo rap, zoo rap, eedle-deedle doo rap!	*(continue dancing)*
I went to the zoo the other day,	*(hold right hand out to side)*
And this is what the animals	*(hold left hand out to side)*
Had to say . . .	*(put both hands to mouth)*
The lion said, "Roar!"	*(place hands at the sides of face and toss head)*
The monkey said, "Hoop!"	*(scratch armpit)*
And the owl said, "Whoo?"	*(hold hands out, palms up and shrug shoulders)*
And, "Hoodle-doodle-doo."	*(swing arms back and forth)*
Zoo rap, zoo rap, hoodle-doodle-doo rap!	*(dance)*
Zoo rap, zoo rap, hoodle-doodle-doo rap!	*(continue dancing)*

Music Selection Collection

Music comes in many different varieties and styles. With so much to choose from, how do you begin to build a library of music that you can use in classroom movement activities? First, choose appropriate music that you like. If you are not enjoying the music, children will notice. Even with suggestions from friends, parents, or "experts," people will never agree on which song or style is best. Second, choose a variety of music. Include songs from various time periods, genres, backgrounds, and tempos. Before going to buy new music, search your own collection. You will probably find several great albums. You can also find music through the local library, friends, parents, and other teachers. Most music and on-line stores allow sampling music before buying it. Performers such as The Beach Boys, Elvis Presley, and the Jackson 5 sing some great wiggling songs. There are also several popular children's performers, such as Drew's Famous Party Music; Joni Bartels; Eddie Coker; Hap Palmer; Raffi; and Sharon, Lois and Bram. Classical music is another important genre that is often used in learning. Classical music is also one of the hardest to buy because many people are not familiar with the titles or composers of often-heard pieces. Below, you will find a good beginner's list of classical titles and a short list of popular albums and collections. Again, you can find these pieces by visiting your local music store or searching on-line stores.

Albinoni, Tomaso Giovanni. "Adagio."
Bach, Johann Sebastian. "Brandenburg" Concerto (Concerto No. 5 in D major: Allegro).
Beethoven, Ludwig van. "Moonlight" Sonata (Piano Sonata No. 14 in C sharp minor).
Bizet, Georges. "March of the Toreadors," Carmen.
Brahms, Johannes. "Cradle Song," Lullaby.
Chopin, Frédéric. "Minute" Waltz (Waltz for piano in D flat major).
Debussy, Claude. "Claire de lune" (Suite bergamasque No. 3, for piano).
Elgar, Edward. "Pomp and Circumstance" (Orchestra March No. 1 in D major).
Gershwin, George. "Rhapsody in Blue."
Grieg, Edvard Hagerup. "Morning," Peer Gynt Suite.
Mendelssohn, Felix. "Wedding March," A Midsummer Night's Dream.
Mouret, Jean-Joseph. "Rondeau."
Mozart, Wolfgang. "Eine kleine Nachtmusik" (Serenade No. 13 for strings in G major: 1st movement).
Offenbach, Jacques. "Operetta Can Can," Orpheus in the Underworld.
Pachelbel, Johann. "Canon in D."
Prokofiev, Sergey. Peter and the Wolf (children's tale for narrator and orchestra).
Ravel, Maurice. "Boléro" (ballet for orchestra or piano).
Rimsky-Korsakov, Nikolay Andreyevich. "The Flight of the Bumblebee," The Tale of Tsar Saltan.
Rossini, Gioacchino. "Largo Al Factorum," The Barber of Seville (opera).
Rossini, Gioacchino. "William Tell" Overture (Finale).
Saint-Saëns, Camille. Carnival of the Animals.
Strauss, Richard. "Sunrise," Also sprach Zarathustra.
Tchaikovsky, Pyotr Ilich. "1812" Festival Overture. (Overture for orchestra in E flat major).
Tchaikovsky, Pyotr Ilich. The Nutcracker Suite (ballet).
Verdi, Giuseppe. "Anvil Chorus," Il Trovatore (opera).
Vivaldi, Antonio. The Four Seasons (Concertos for violin).

Albums, Collections

A Child's Celebration of Dance Music. Music Little People, 1998. ASIN: B00000AFXQ.
A Child's Celebration of Rock 'n' Roll. Music Little People, 1996. ASIN: B000002M7T.
Classics for Children by Arthur Fiedler and the Boston Pops. RCA, 1995. ASIN: B000003FVT.
For the Kids. Nettwerk Records, 2002. ASIN: B00006L7QX.
Funny 50's & Silly 60's by The Re-Bops. Re-Bop Records, 2000. ASIN: B00000AG5V.
Pavarotti's Opera Made Easy—My Favorite Opera for Children. Decca, 1994. ASIN: B00000424Y.
Smithsonian Folkways Children's Music Collection. Smithsonian Folkways, 1998. ASIN: B000001DOB.
World Playground by Putumayo Presents (Series). Putumayo World Music, 1999. ASIN: B00000JT4P.